Finding Hawaii

Artistic Images of Objects Found Around Hawaii... To Color!

Brittney Kauffman

Copyright © 2018 by Brittney Kauffman

All rights reserved.
This book or any portion thereof
may not be reproduced or used in any manner
whatsoever without the express written permission of
the artist.

First Printing, 2018

ISBN-10 1727238931

www.facebook.com/artbybrittneyk
inkedfoxak@gmail.com

Guidelines

1. Gently tear or cut the page of your choosing out of the coloring book.
2. Color your page using colored pencils, fine-tip markers, or fine-tip pens. It's your art, so these are just suggestions. (I personally use Staedtler marker pens)
3. Find the word 'Hawaii' hidden in your drawing.
4. Display! Each page is 8x10 and one-sided for the purpose of being able to display your work, should you choose to do so. (8x10 is also a standard frame size)

Most of all, have fun!

Can't find 'Hawaii' in your drawing? Look to the back of the book for help!

This coloring book is dedicated to my daughter, Charlotte, and my partner, Jerrid, for helping me find the time to get this done.

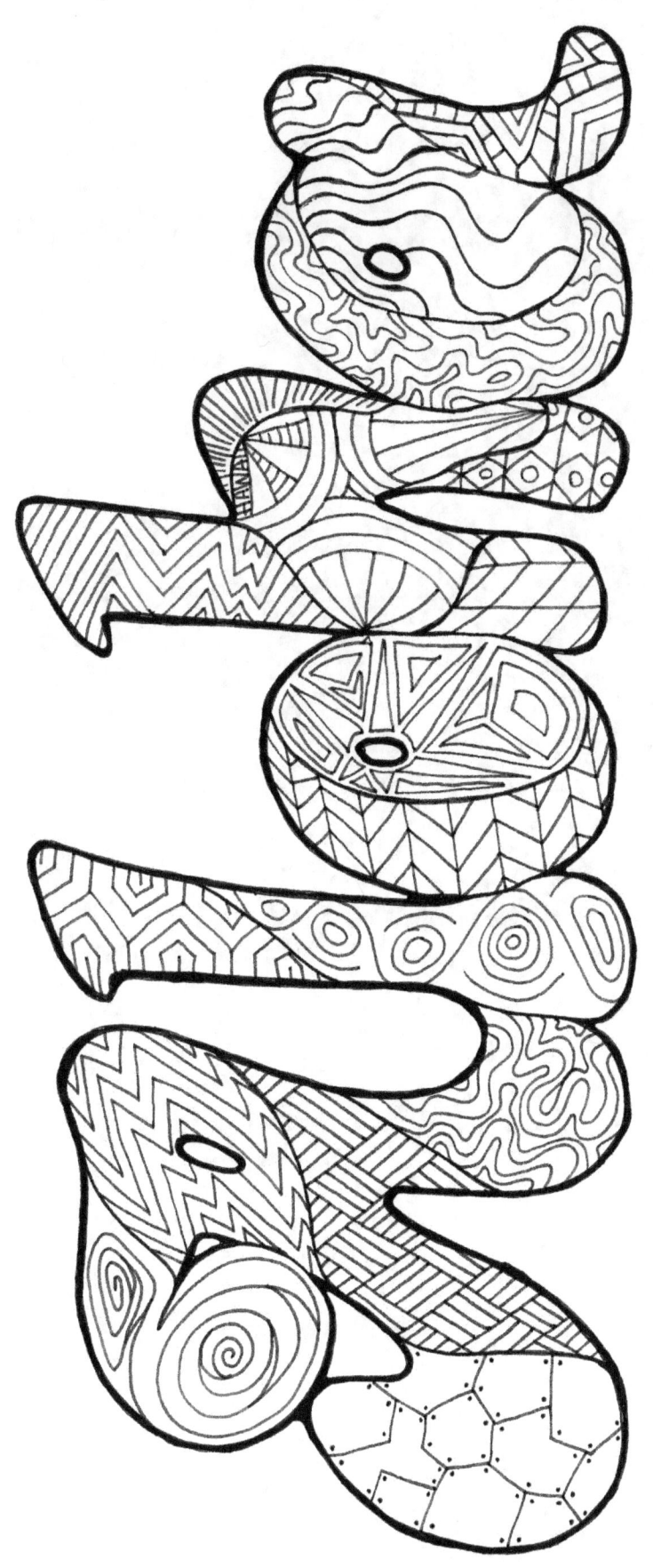

Aloha

A greeting or goodbye in Hawaii

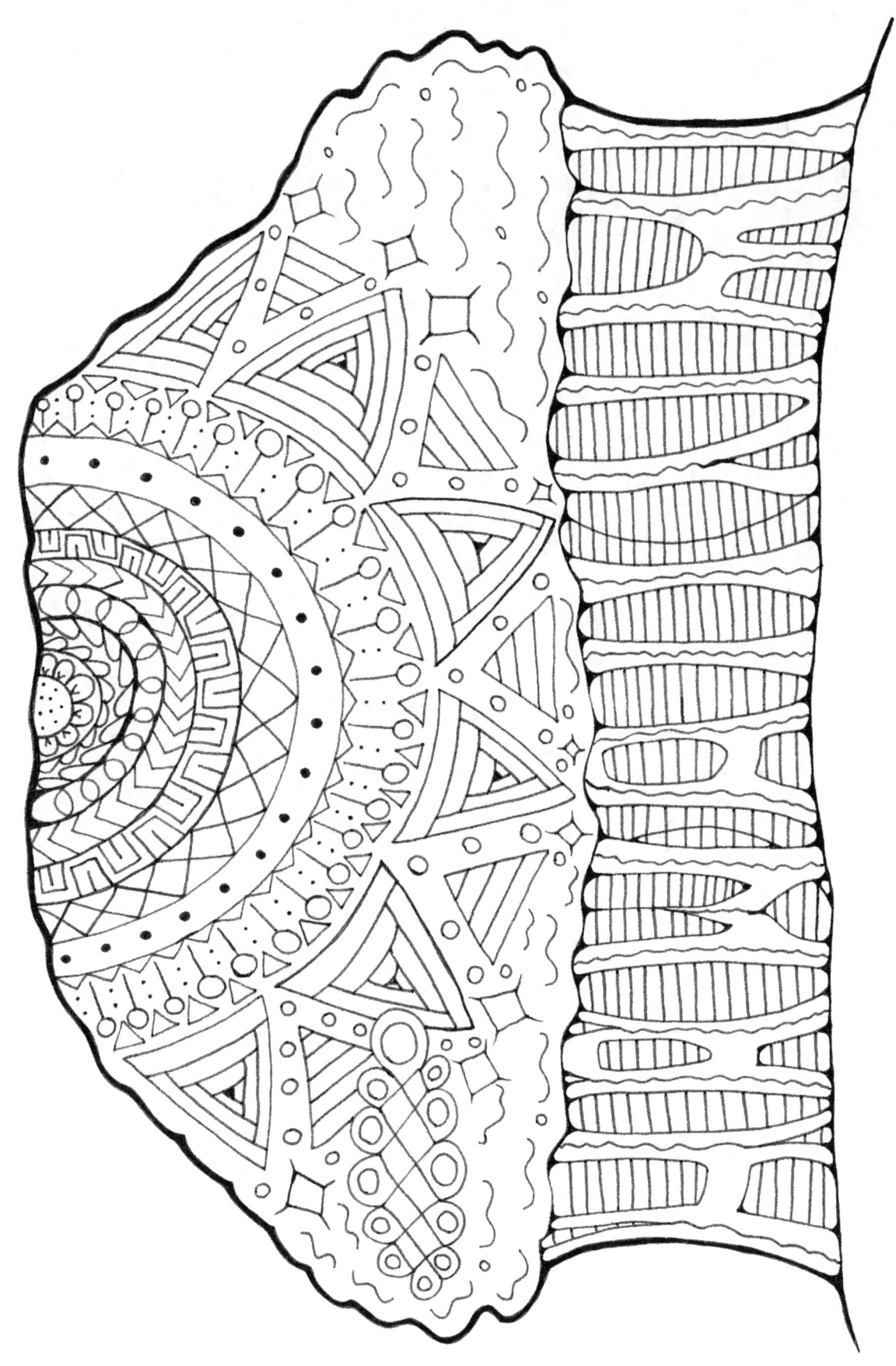

Banyan Tree

The Banyan tree is a species of fig tree

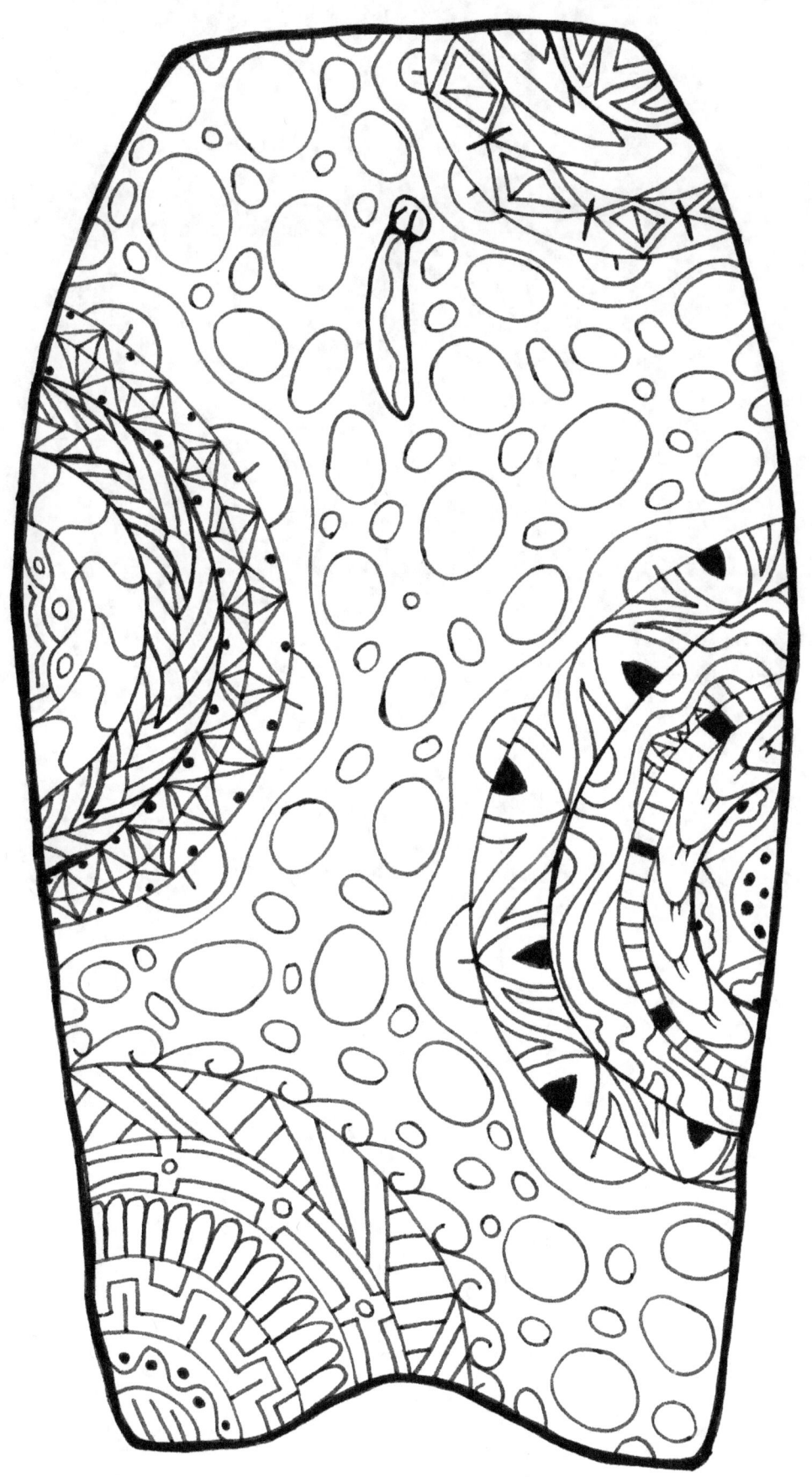

Boogie Board

Boogie boarding is a fun pastime in Hawaii

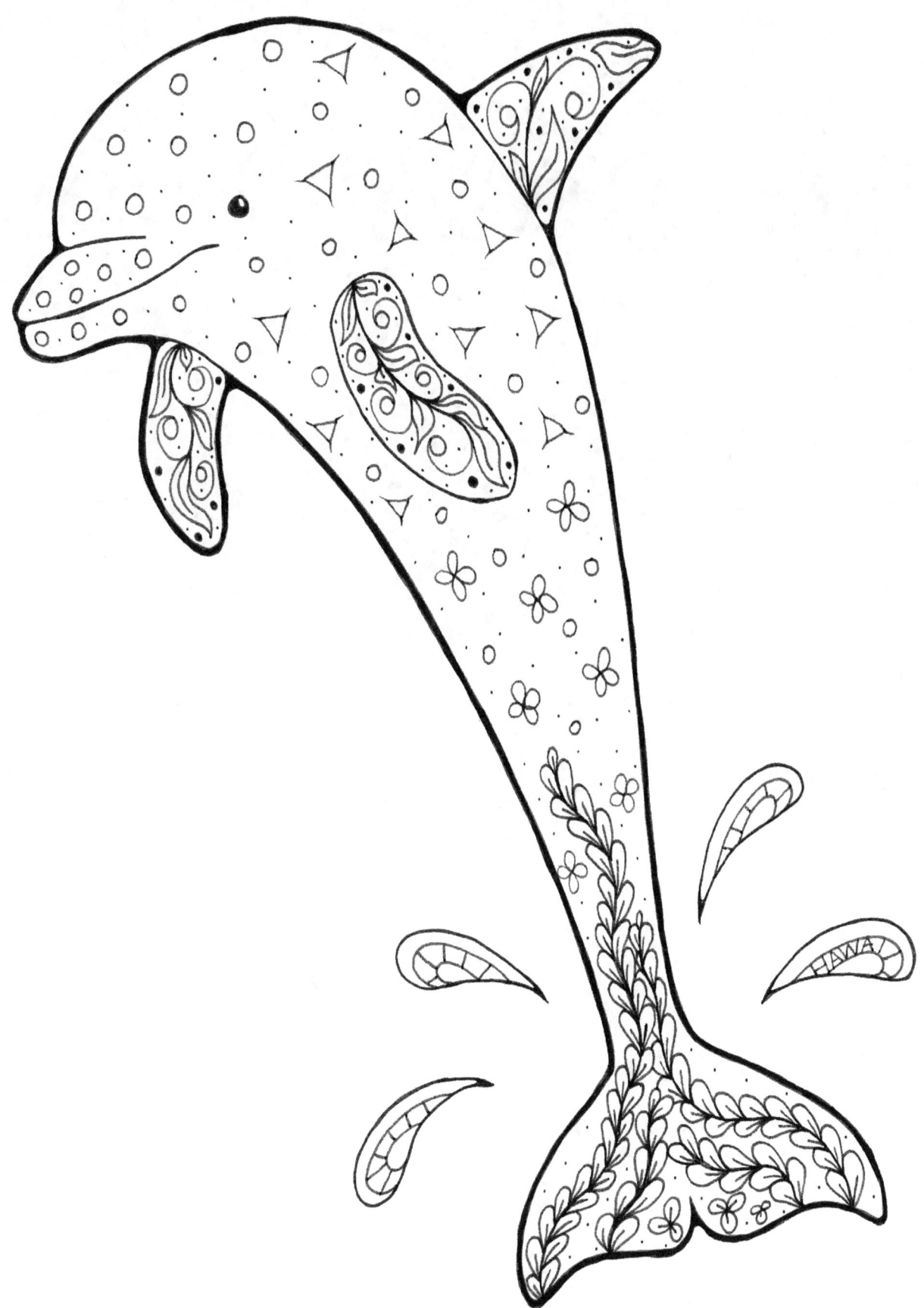

Bottlenose Dolphin

Bottlenose dolphins are one type of dolphin commonly seen
In Hawaii

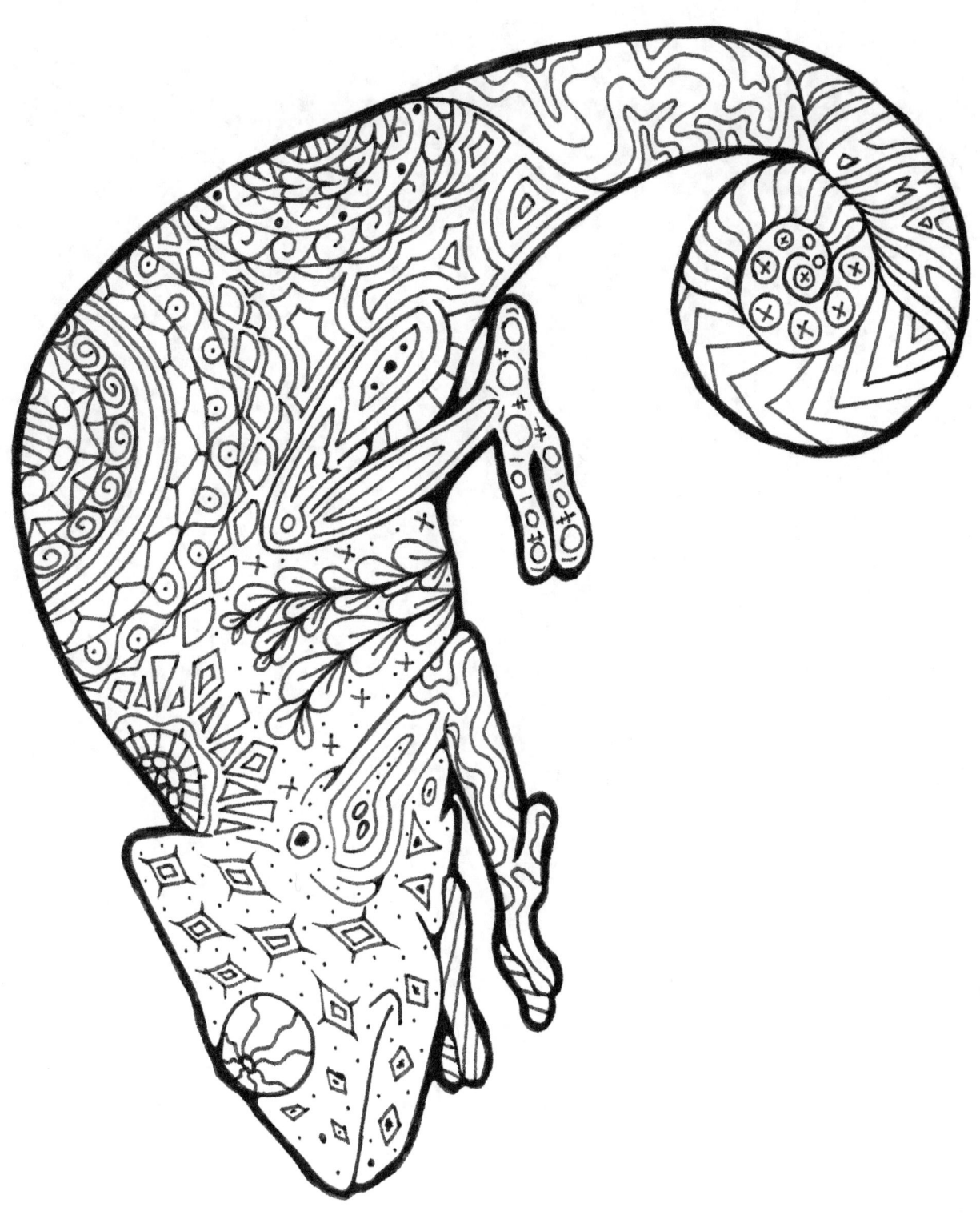

Veiled Chameleon

A female veiled chameleon can lay 30-95 eggs in a hole in the ground up to three times a year

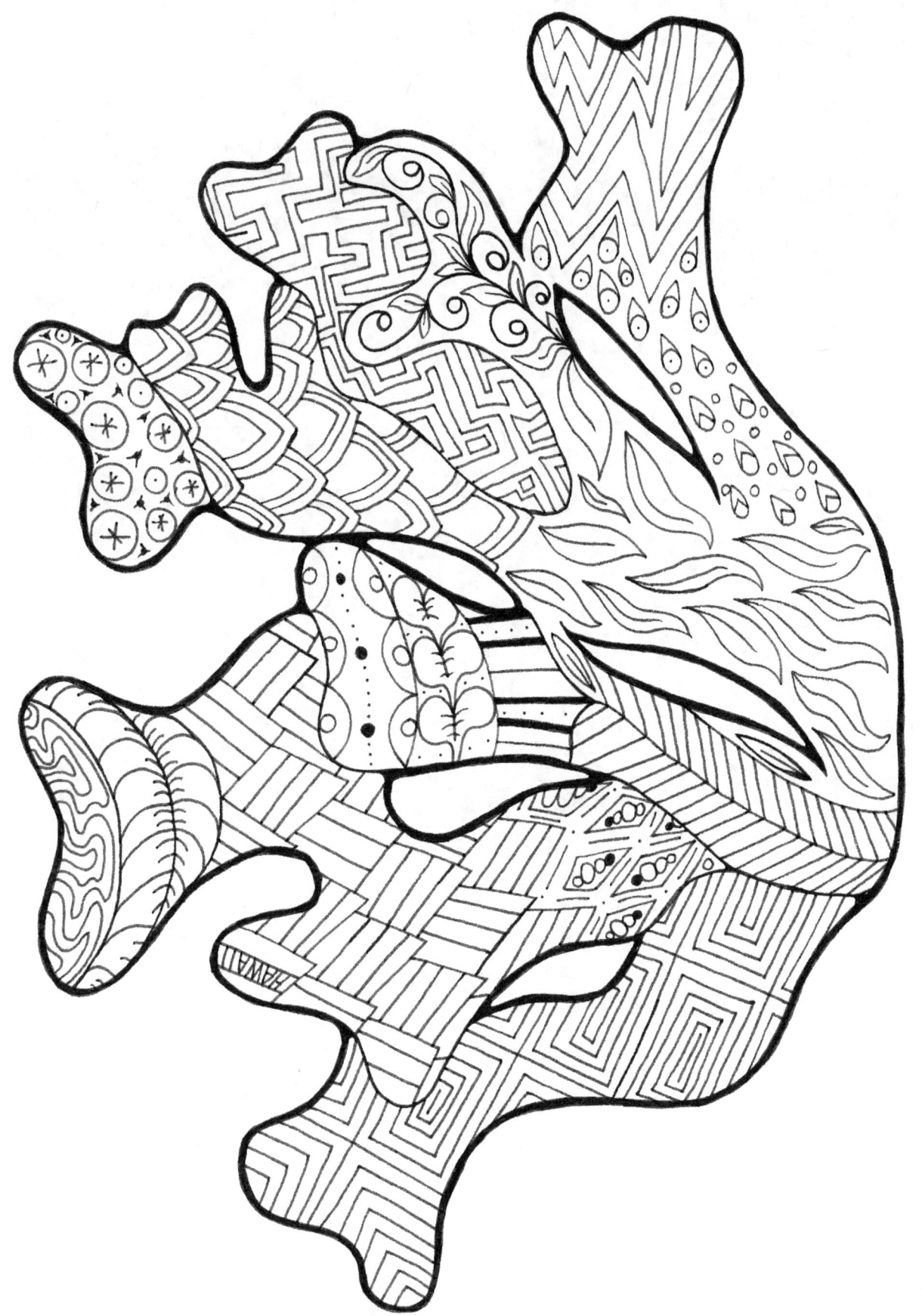

Coral

Over 500 species live in the coral reefs around Hawaii

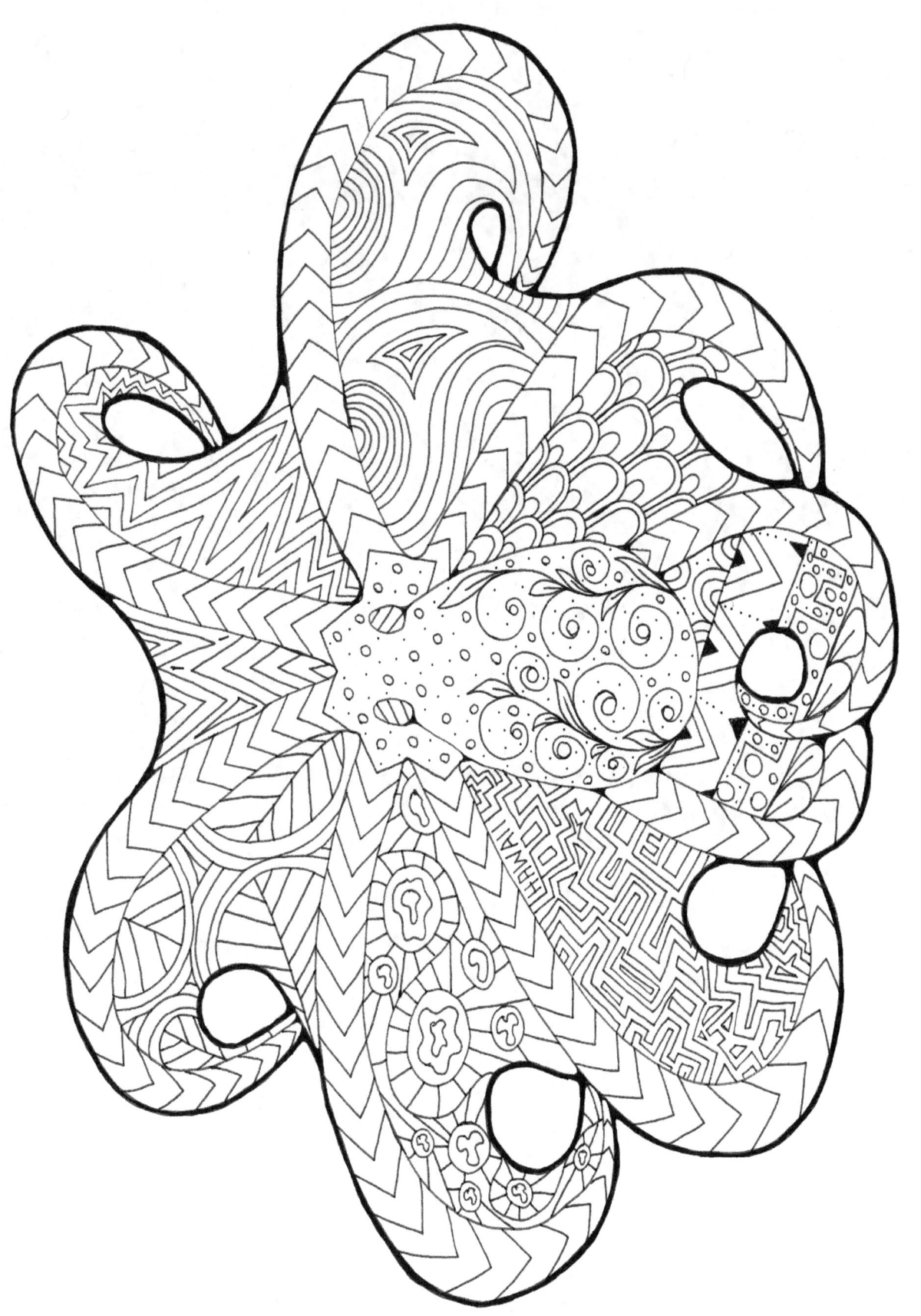

Day Octopus

Of the family *Octopodidae*

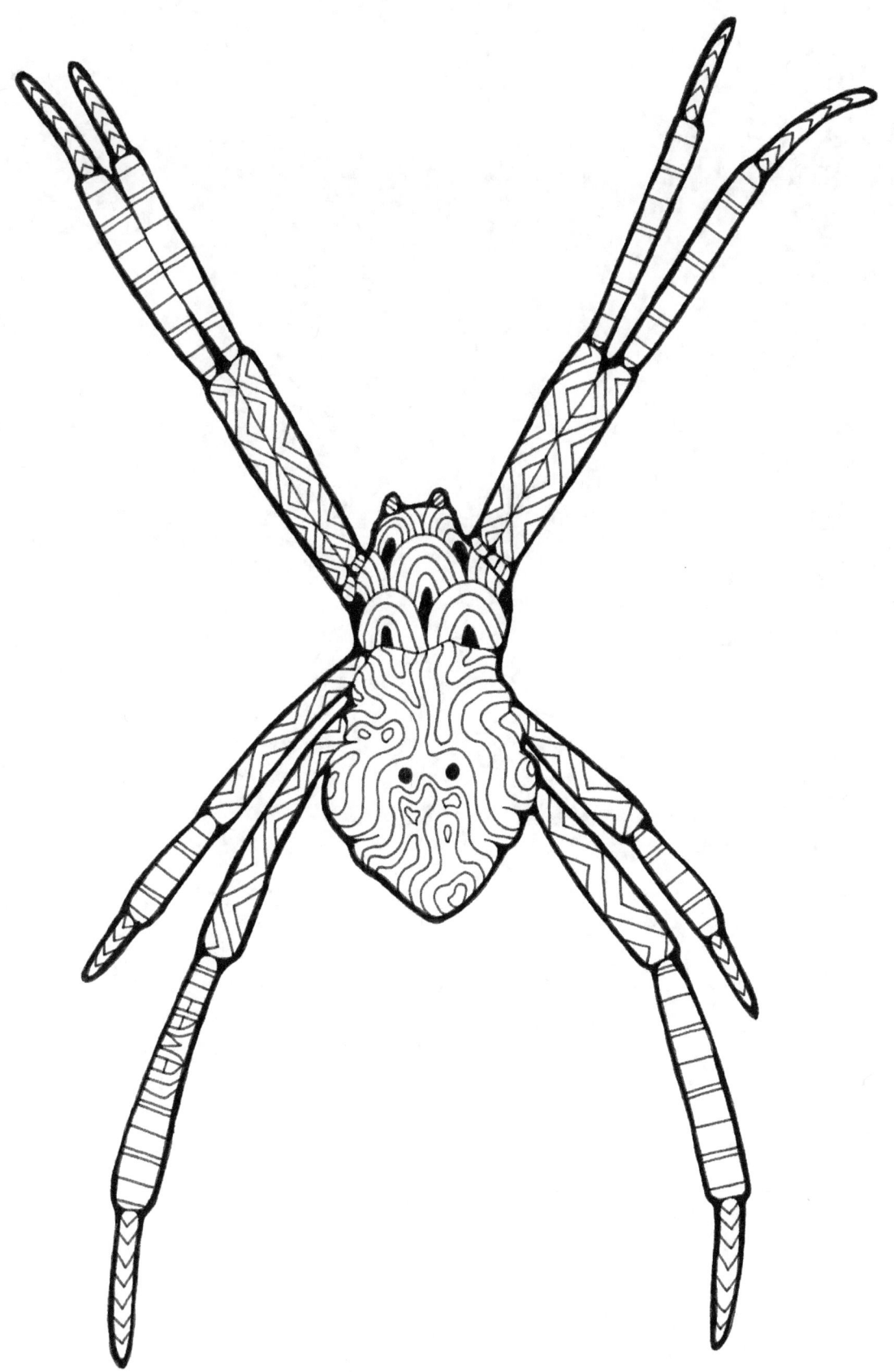

Garden Spider

Common spider in Hawaii; not poisonous to humans

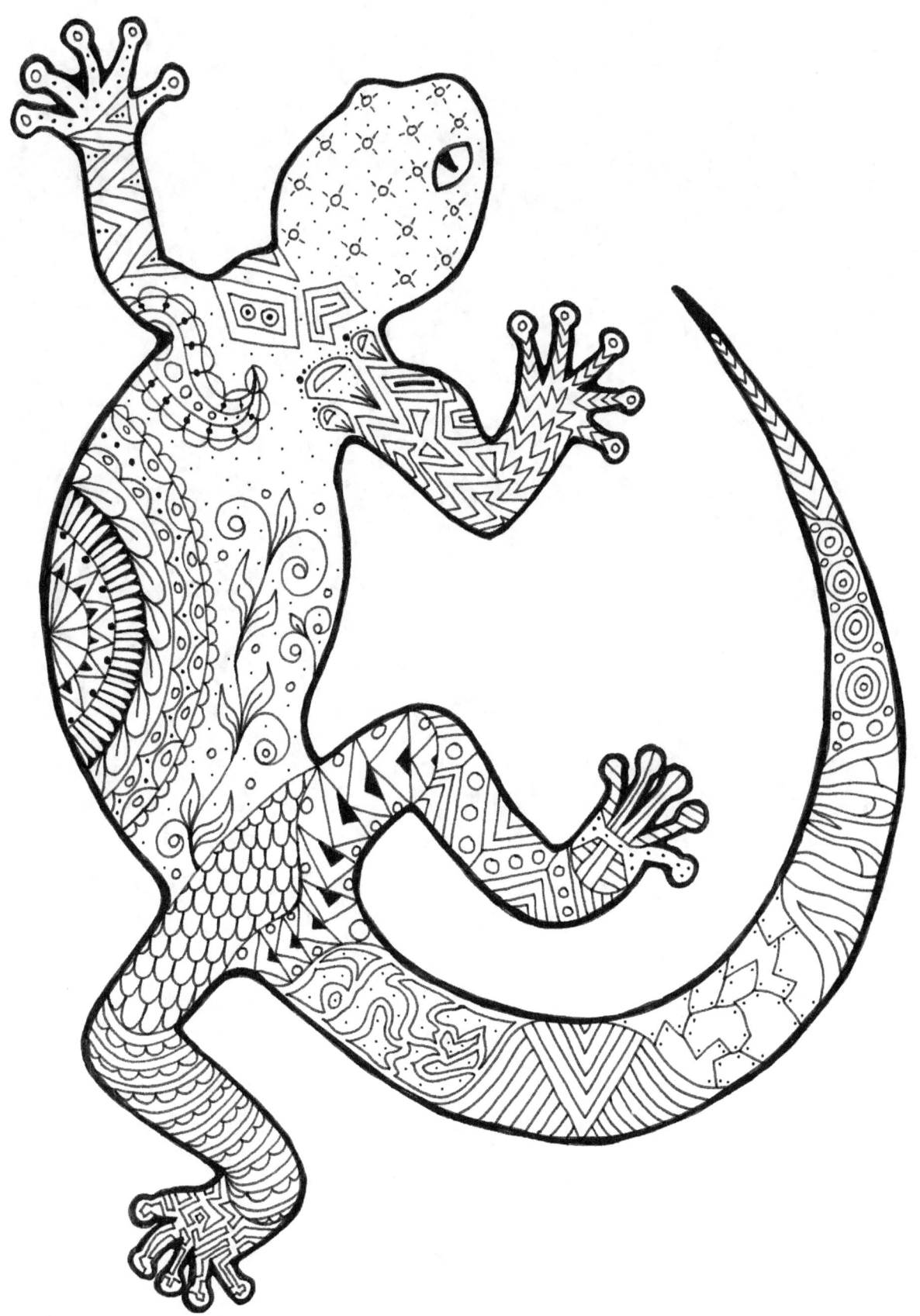

Gecko

A gecko can regrow its tail within weeks

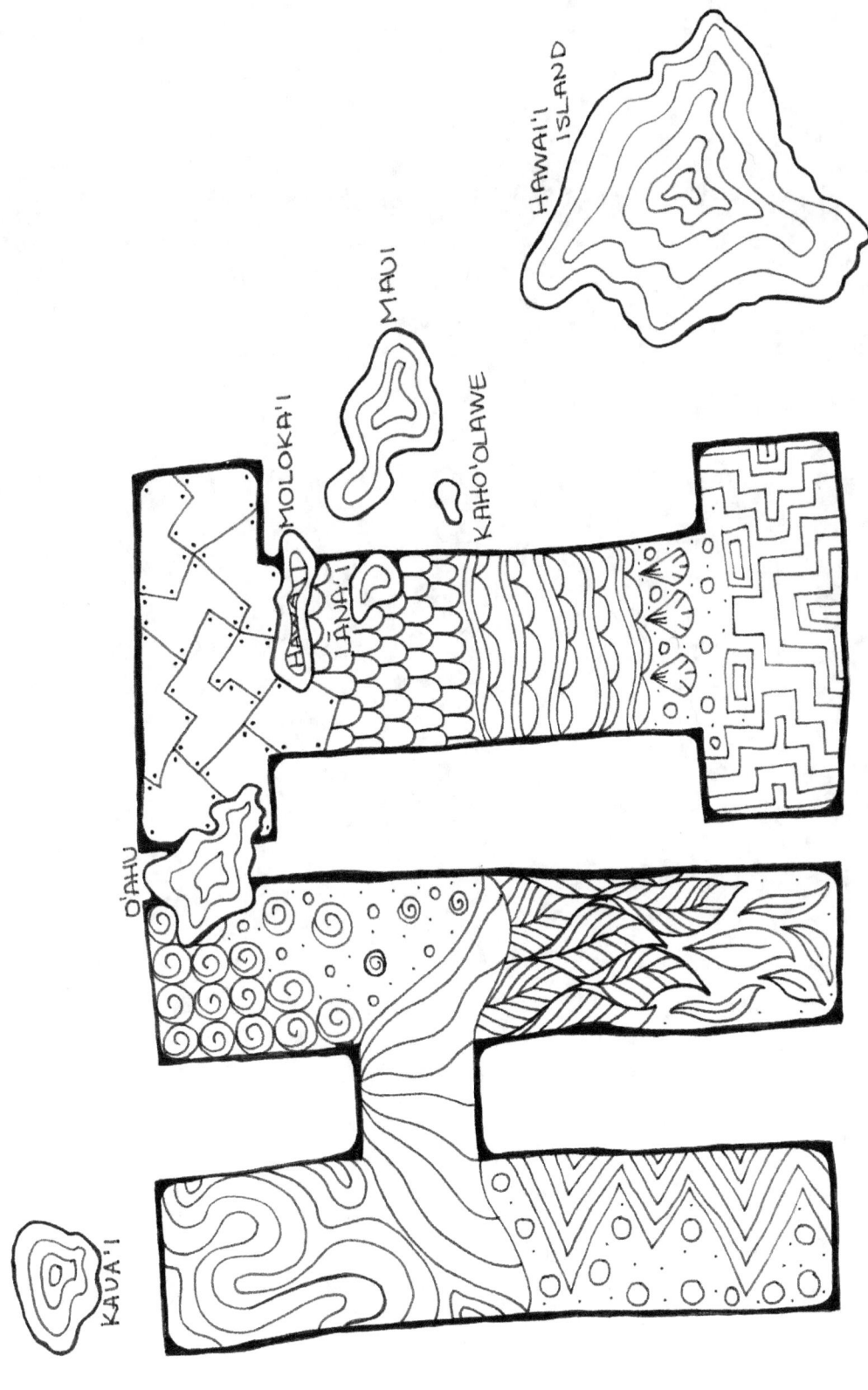

Hawai'i Islands

The eight major Hawaiian islands are: Hawai'i, Maui, O'ahu, Kaua'i, Moloka'i, Lāna'i, Ni'ihau, and Kaho'olawe. These are in order of largest island to smallest.

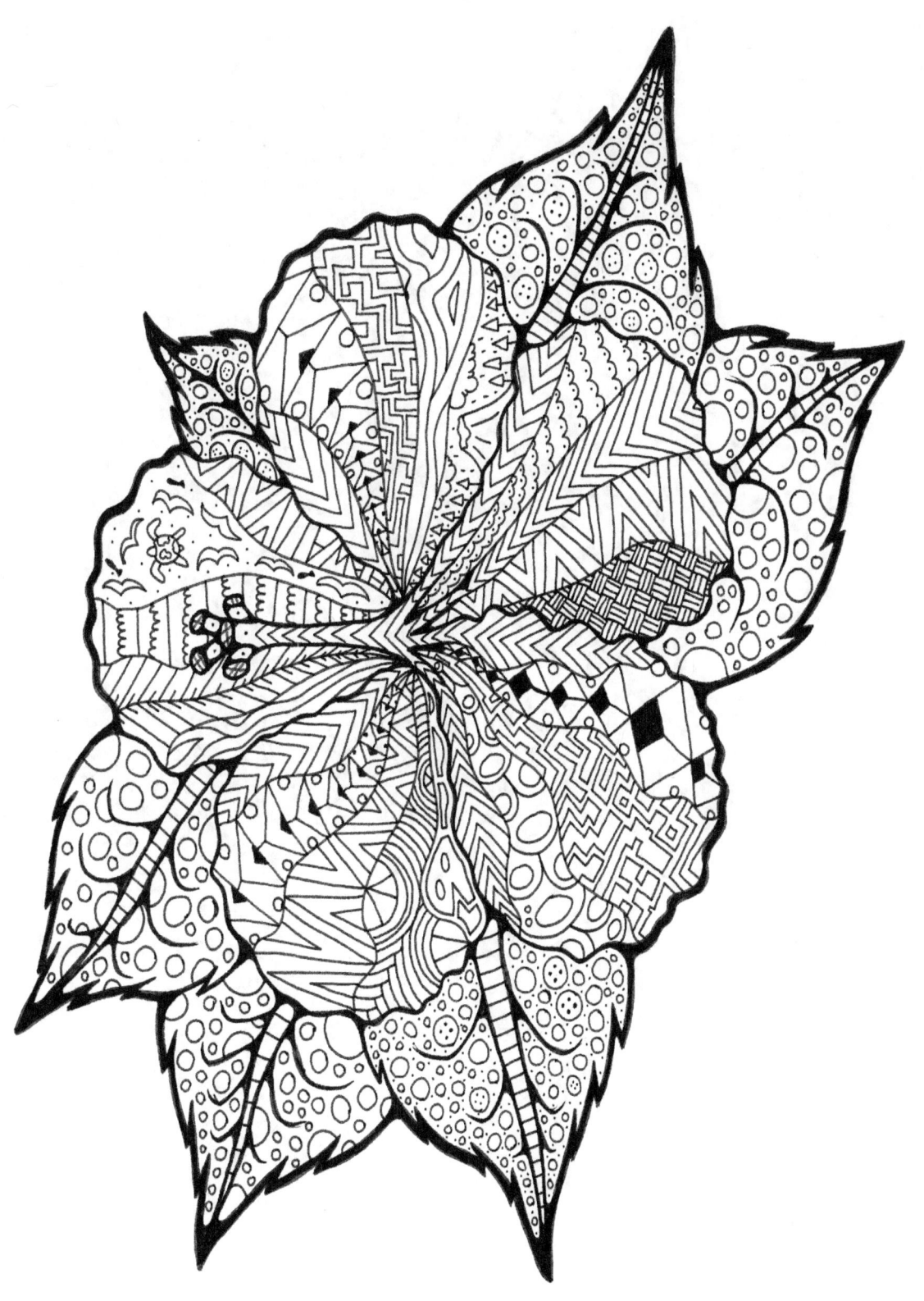

Hibiscus Flower

The yellow hibiscus is the state flower of Hawaii

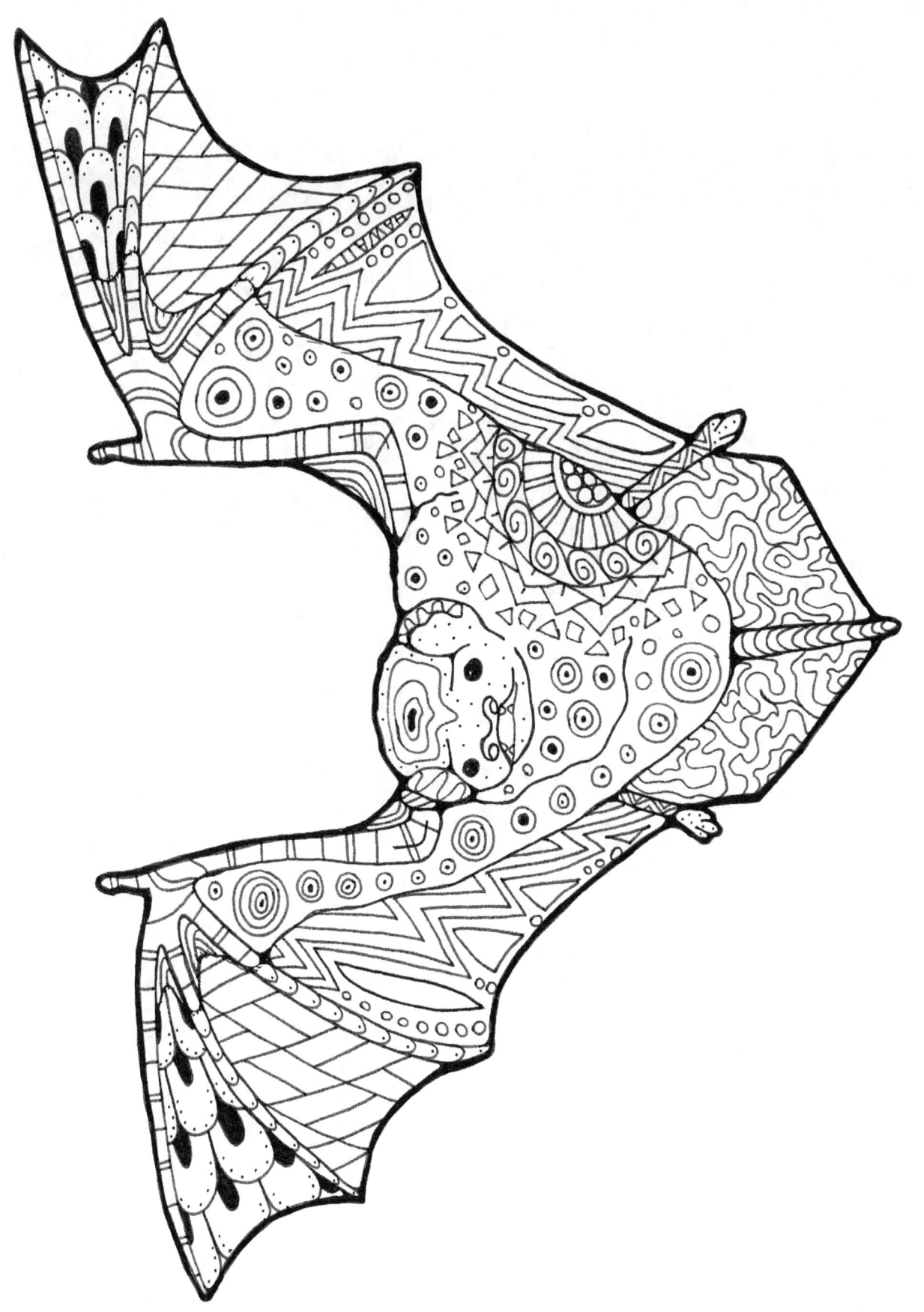

Hawaiian Hoary Bat

The Hawaiian hoary bat has been on the endangered species list since 1970

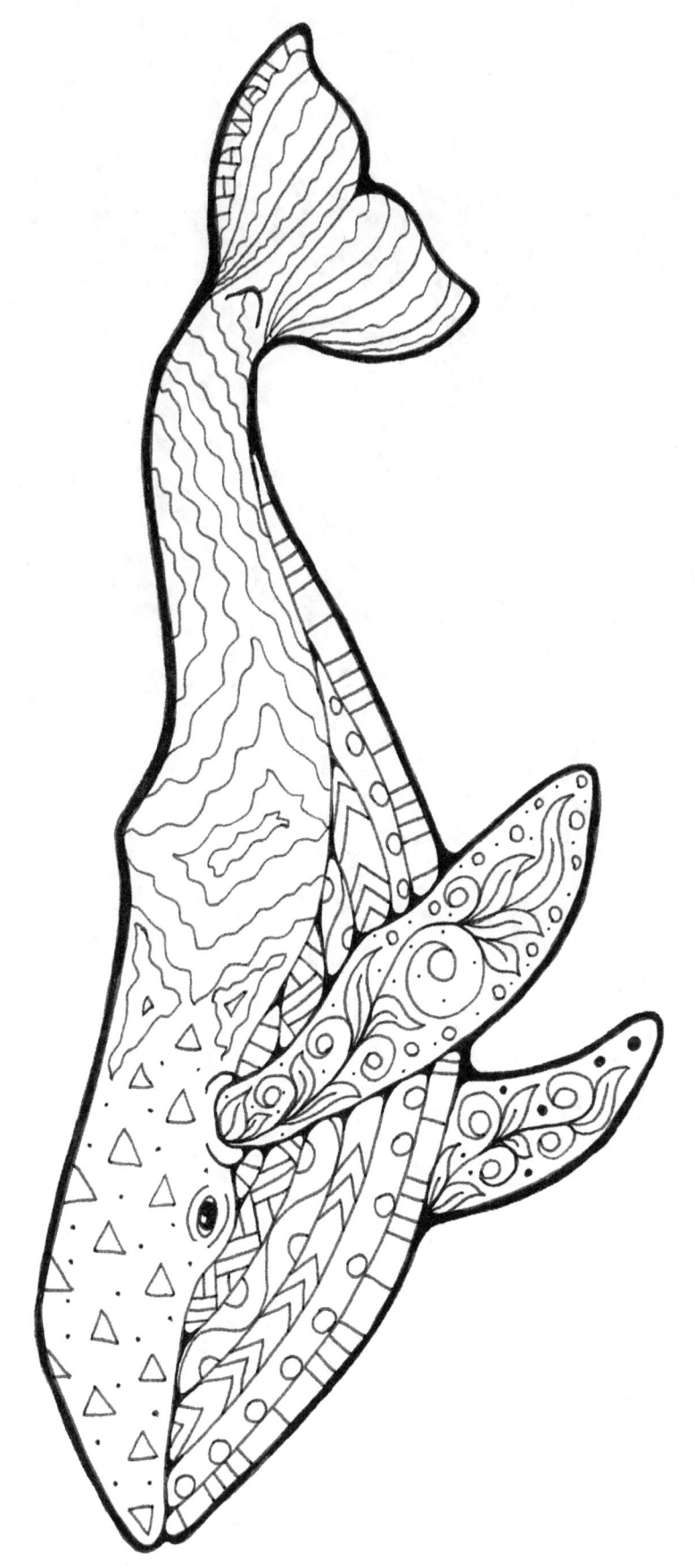

Humpback Whale

Humpback whales like to winter near the Hawaiian Islands; breeding and calving in the warmer waters

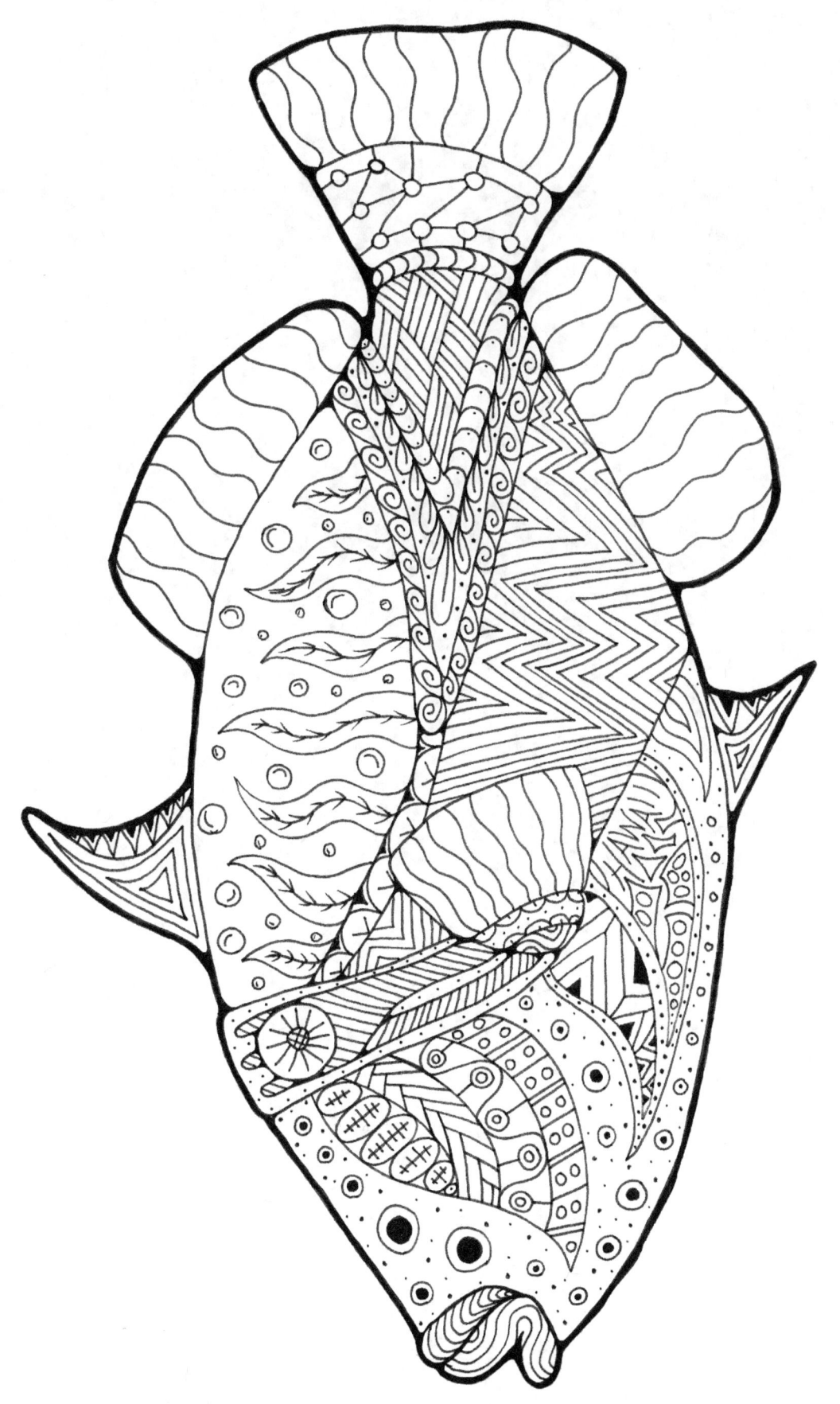

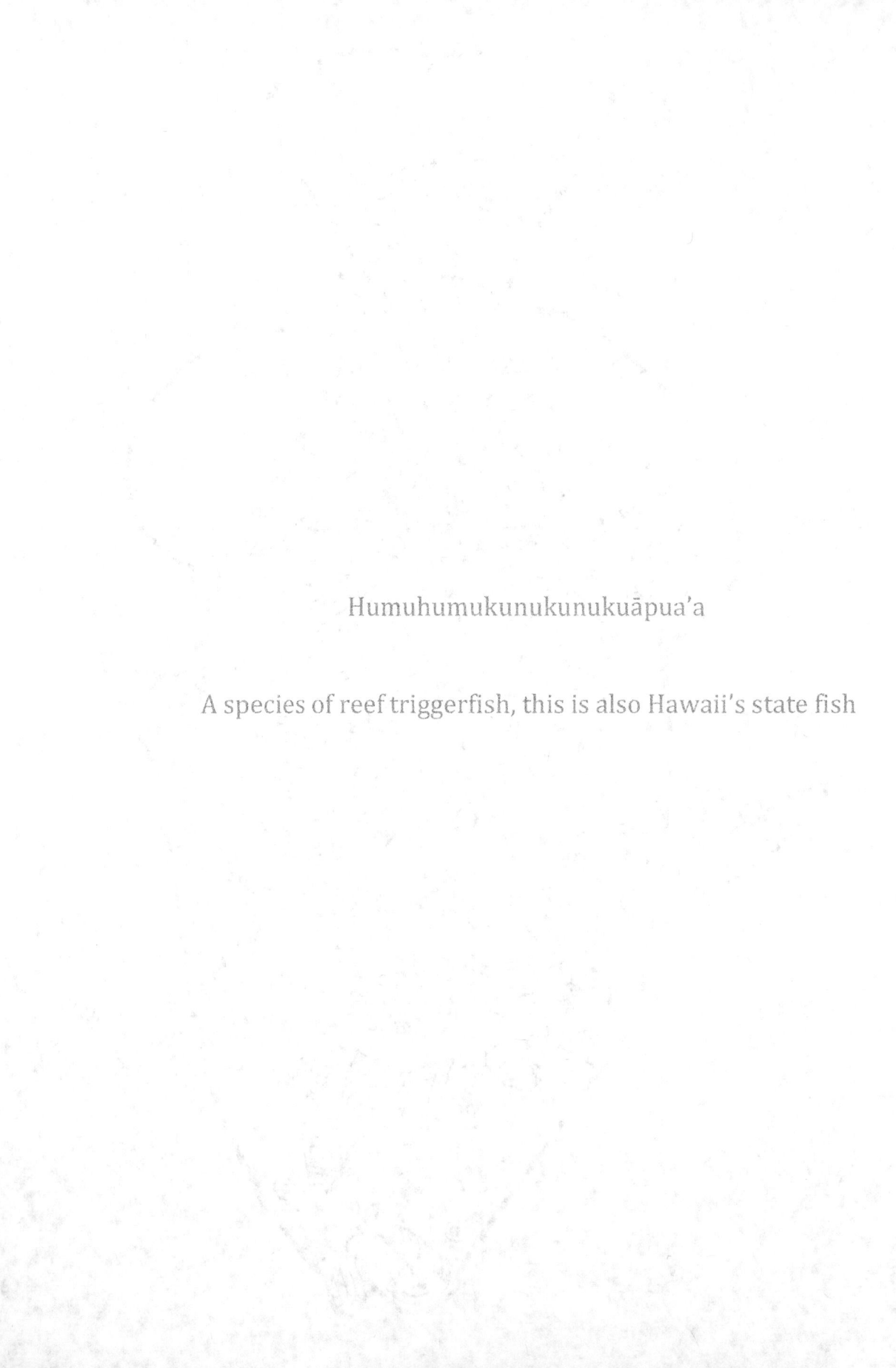

Humuhumukunukunukuāpua'a

A species of reef triggerfish, this is also Hawaii's state fish

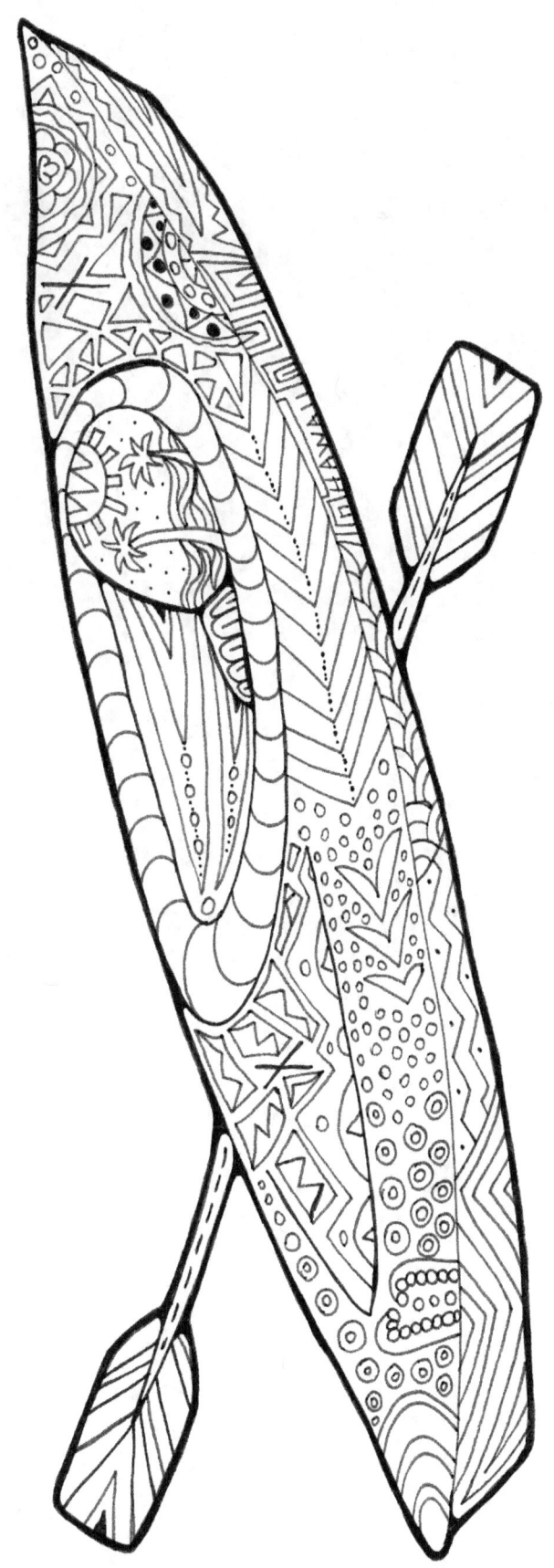

Kayaking in Hawaii

Kayaking is another enjoyable pastime in Hawaii

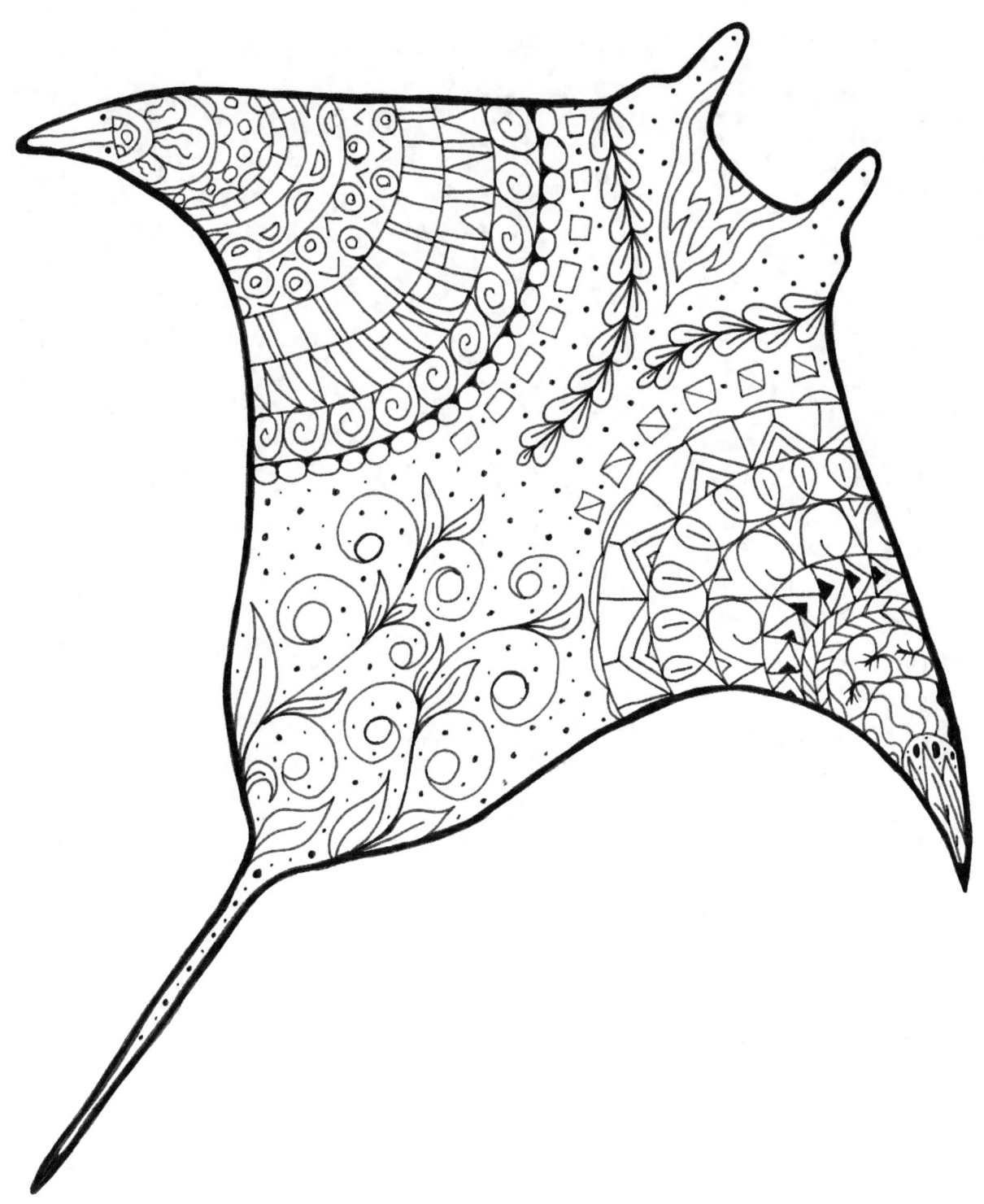

Manta Ray

The offspring of the manta ray are known as "pups"

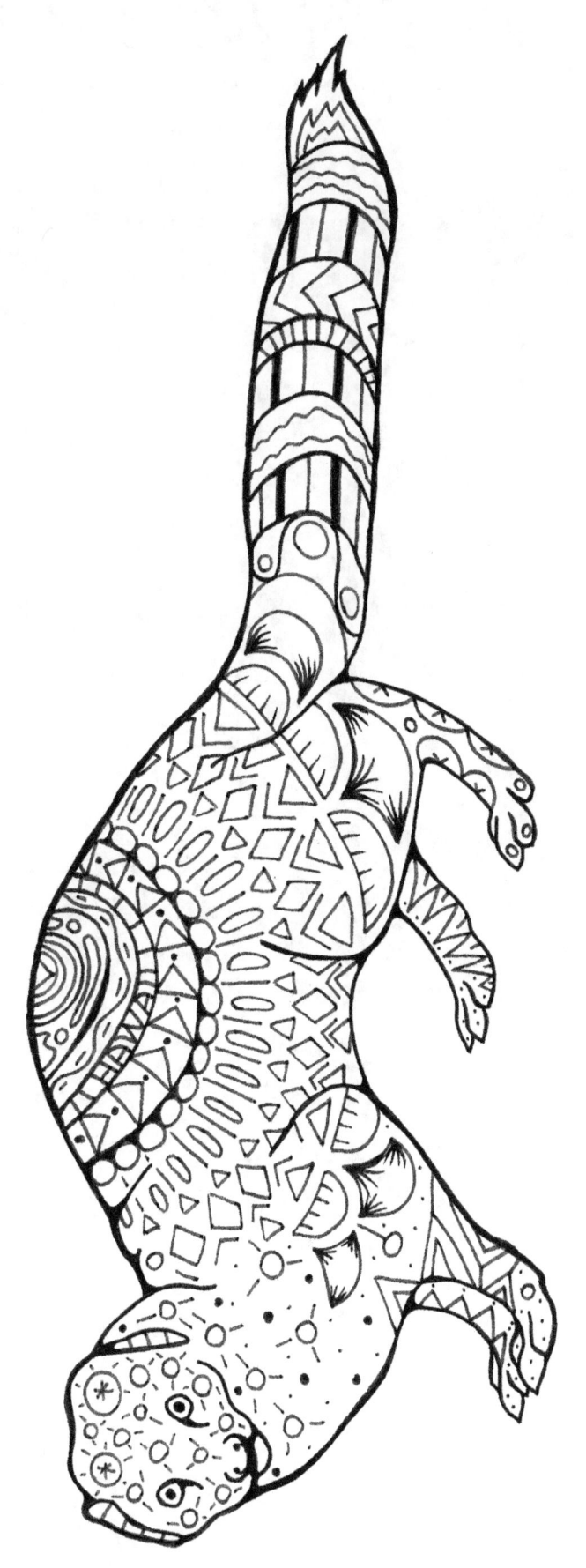

Mongoose

Mongooses are "diurnal," meaning they are active during the day

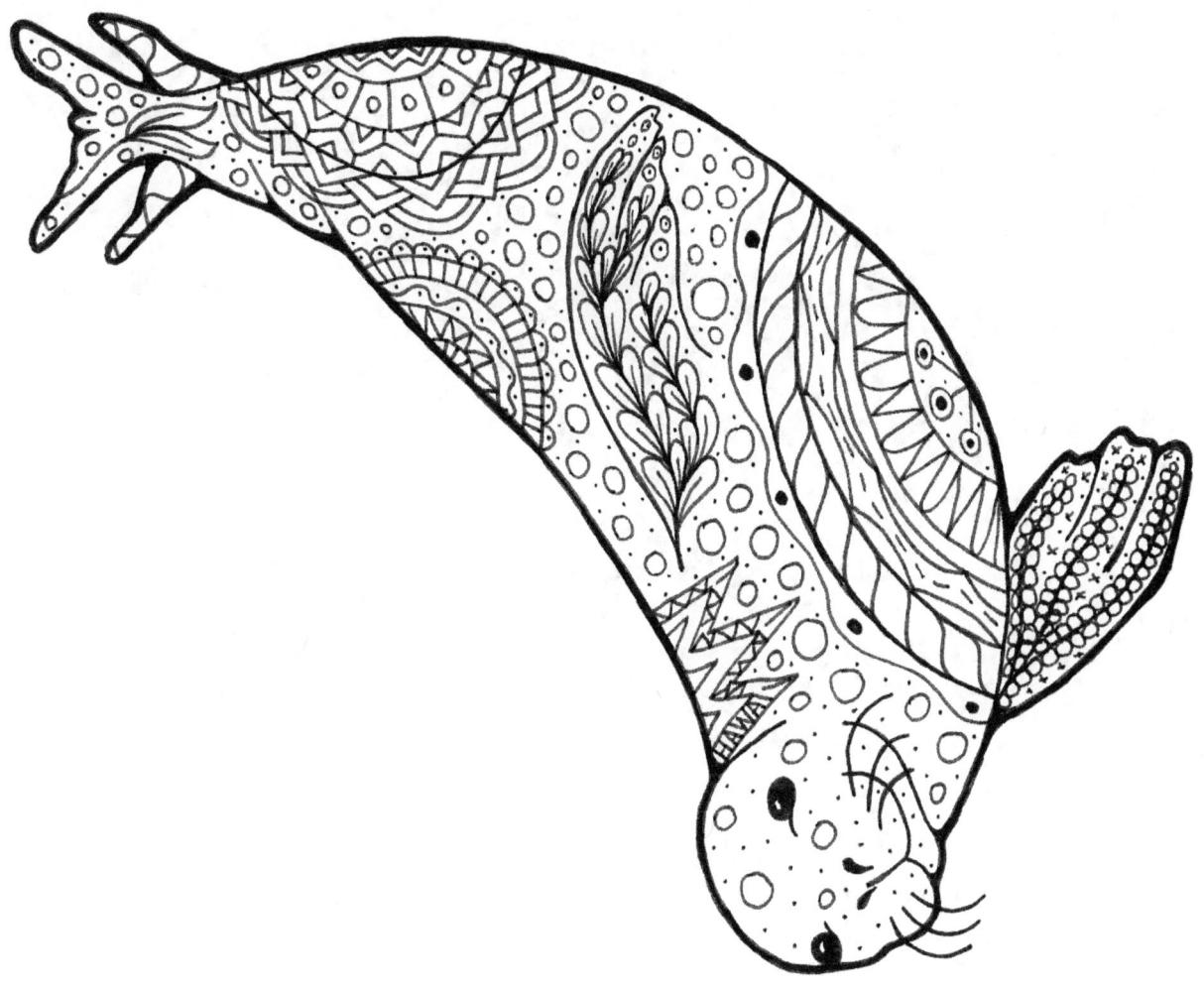

Hawaiian Monk Seal

The Hawaiian monk seal is an endangered species, and also the state mammal of Hawaii

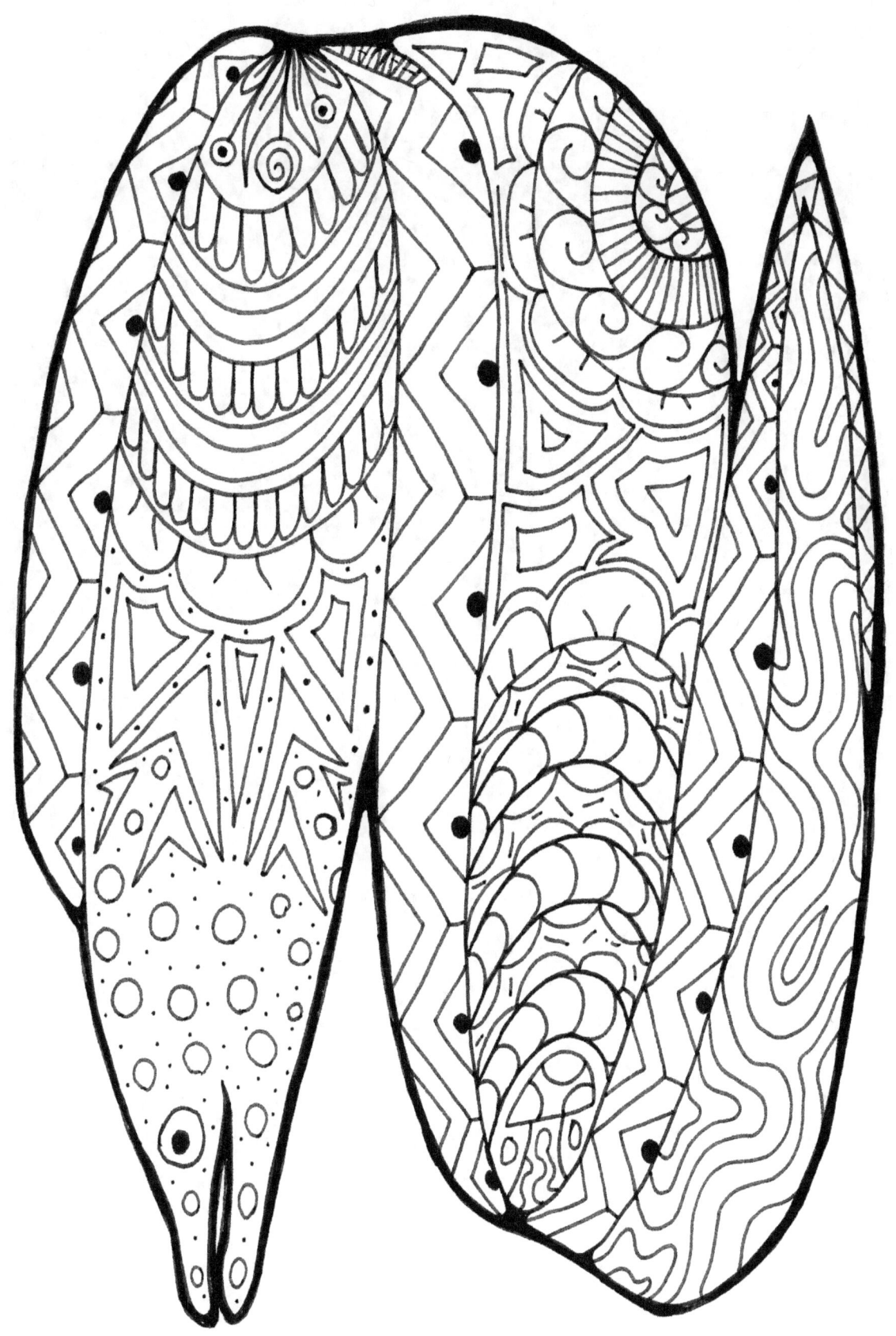

Moray Eel

Moray Eel are called "puhi" in Hawaiian

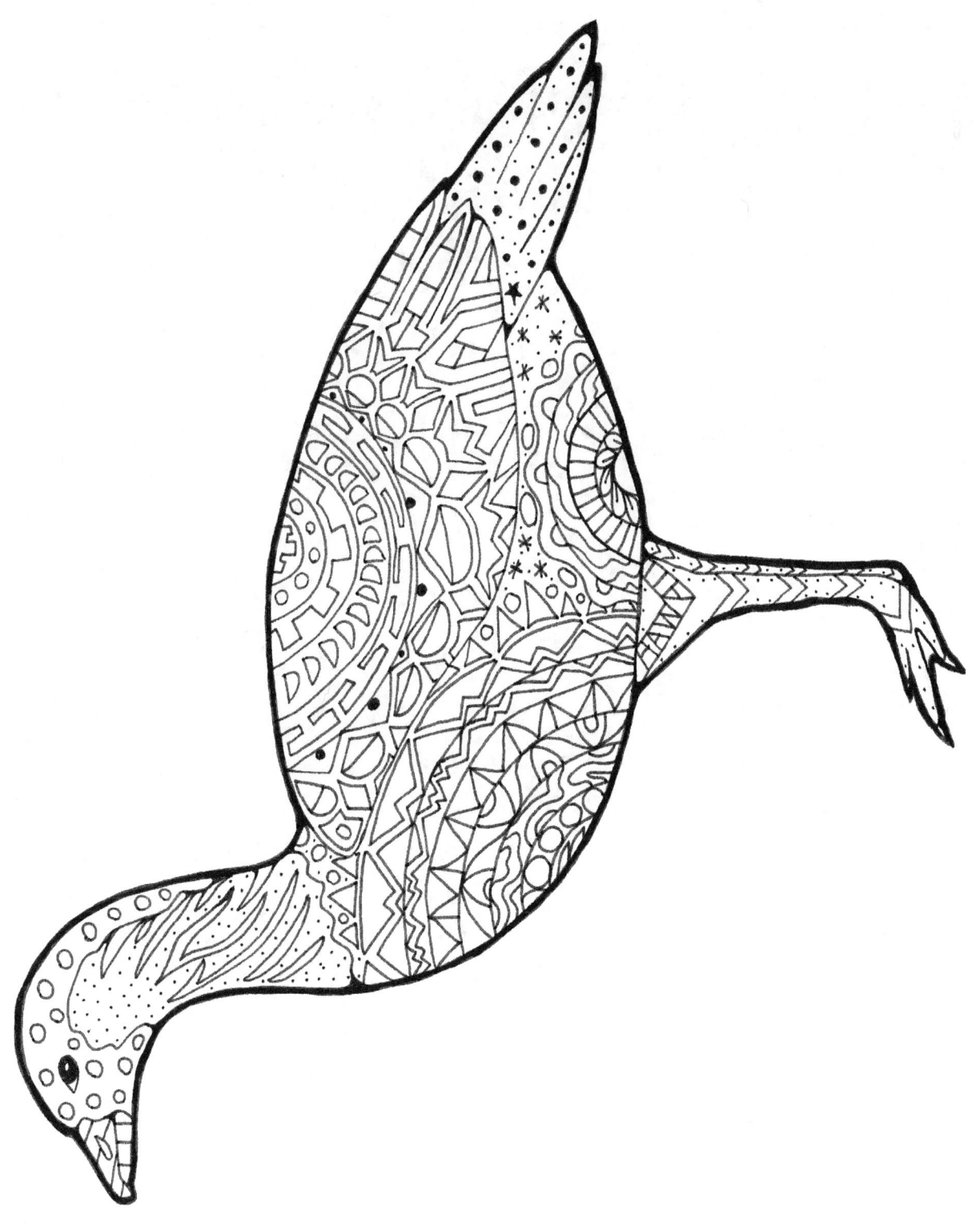

Nene

The Nene is the state bird of Hawaii

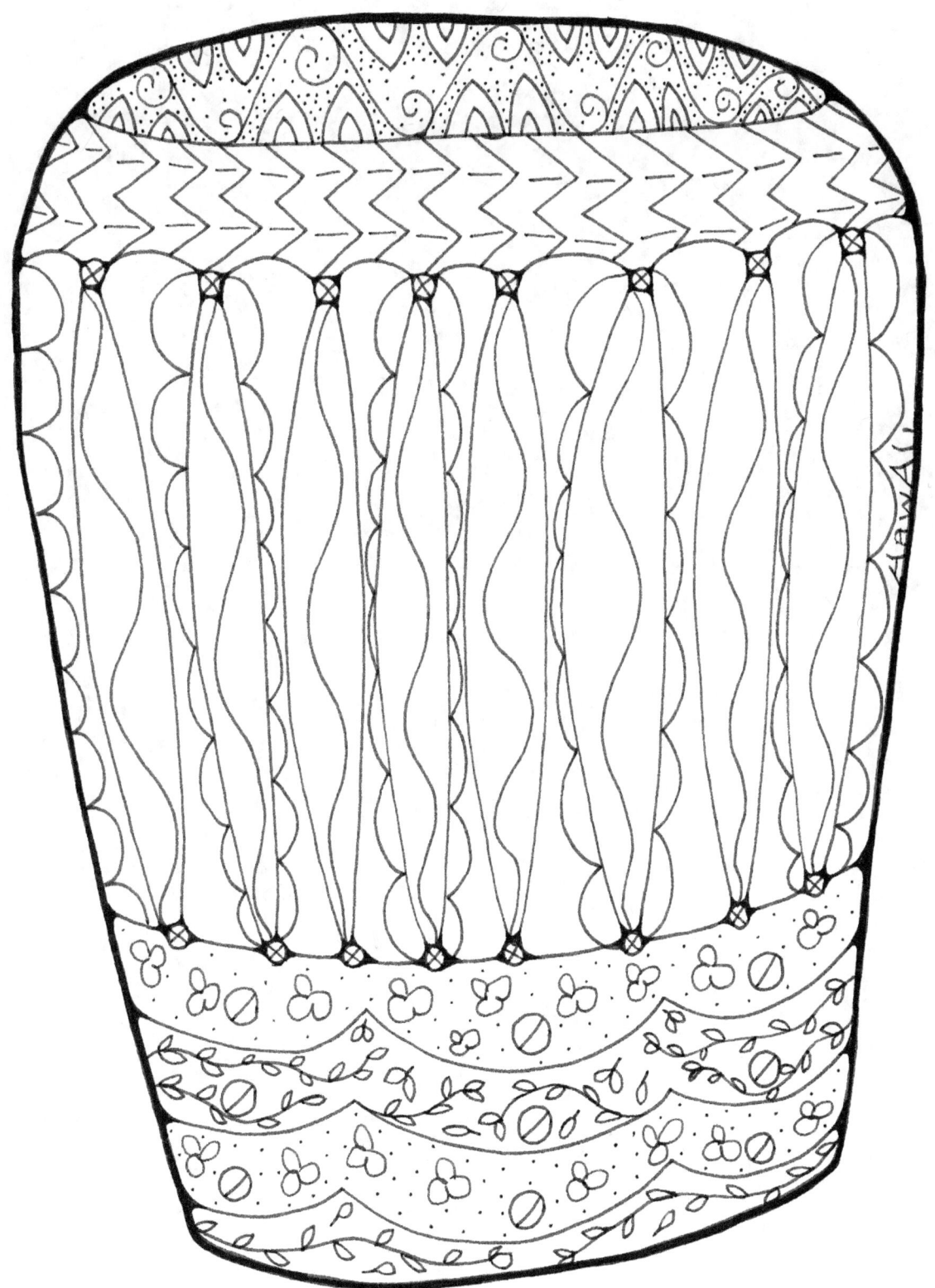

Pahu

Pahu means "drum" in Hawaiian and is used for religious ceremonies and hula

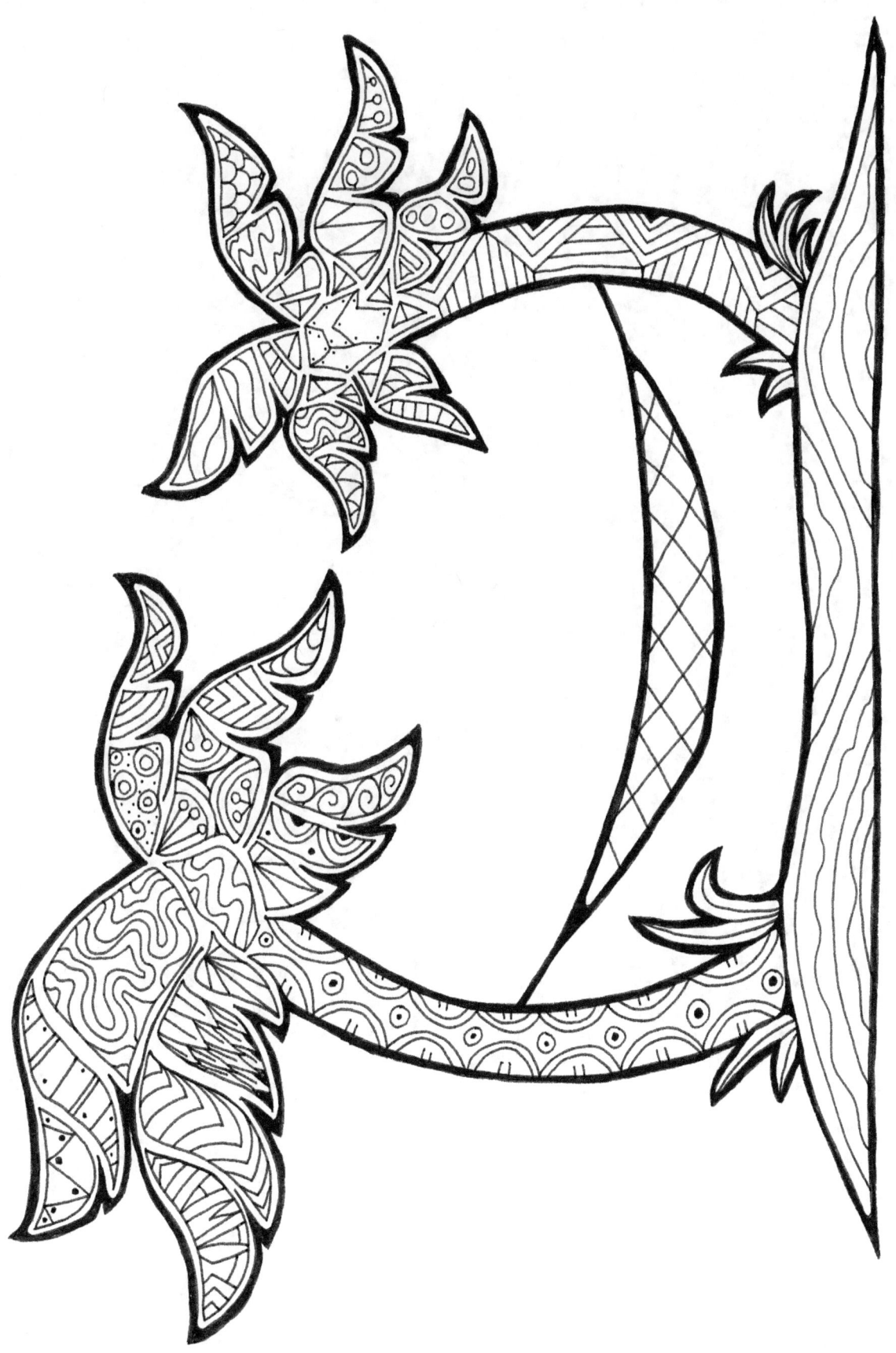

Palm Trees with Hammock

The Loulu Palm is the only native palm tree to Hawaii

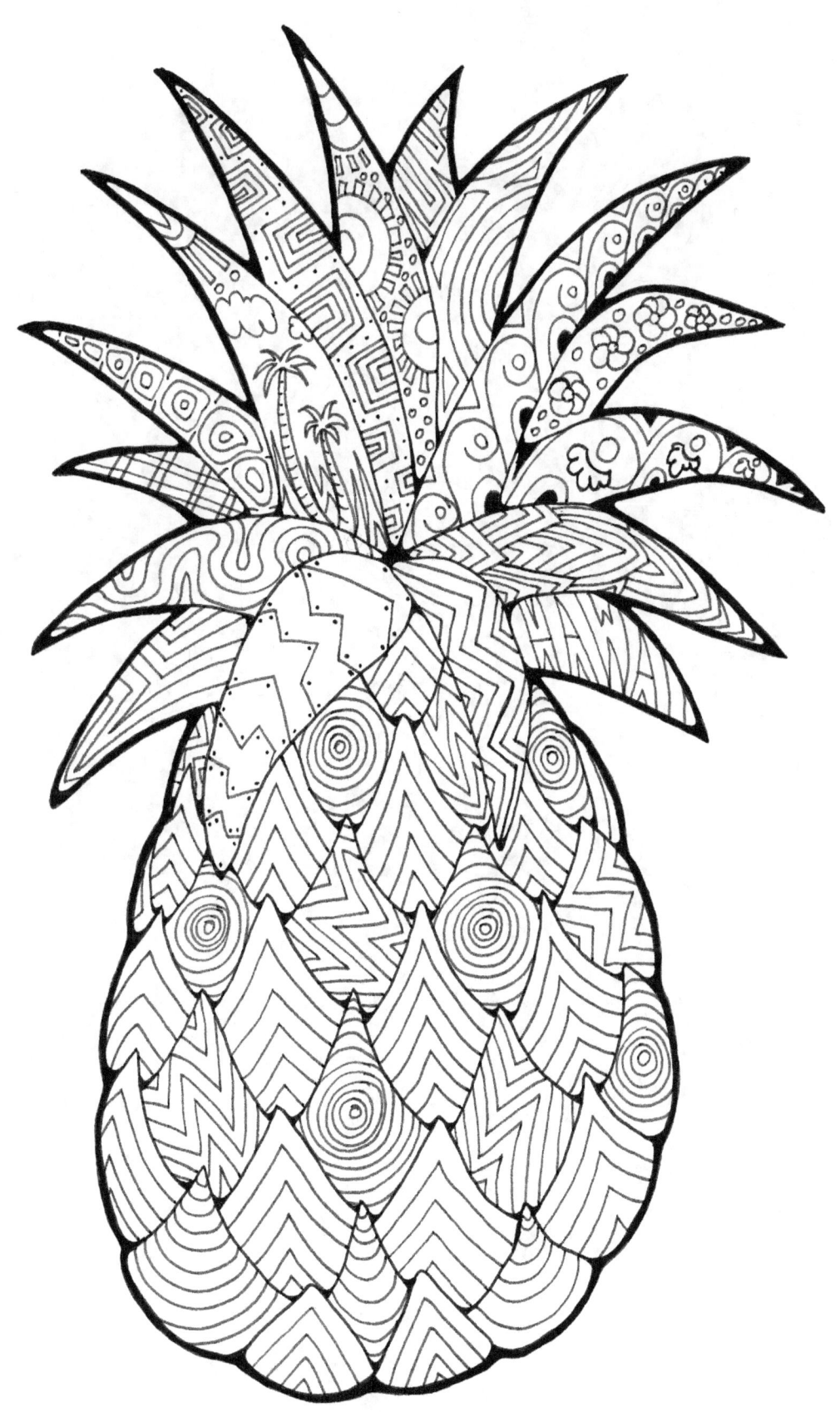

Pineapple

Pineapples are called "hala kahiki" in Hawaiian

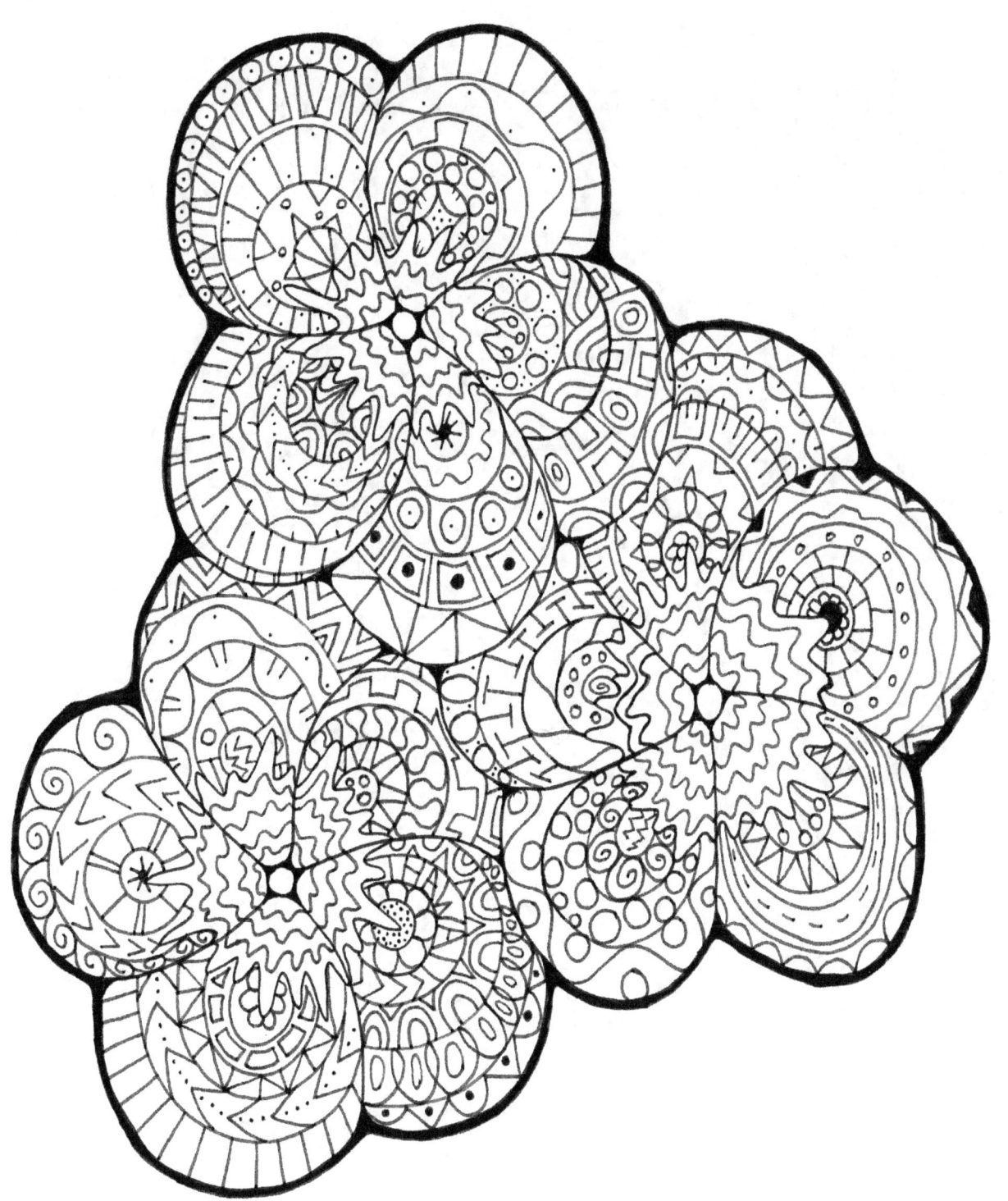

Plumeria

Plumerias are commonly used to make leis in Hawaii

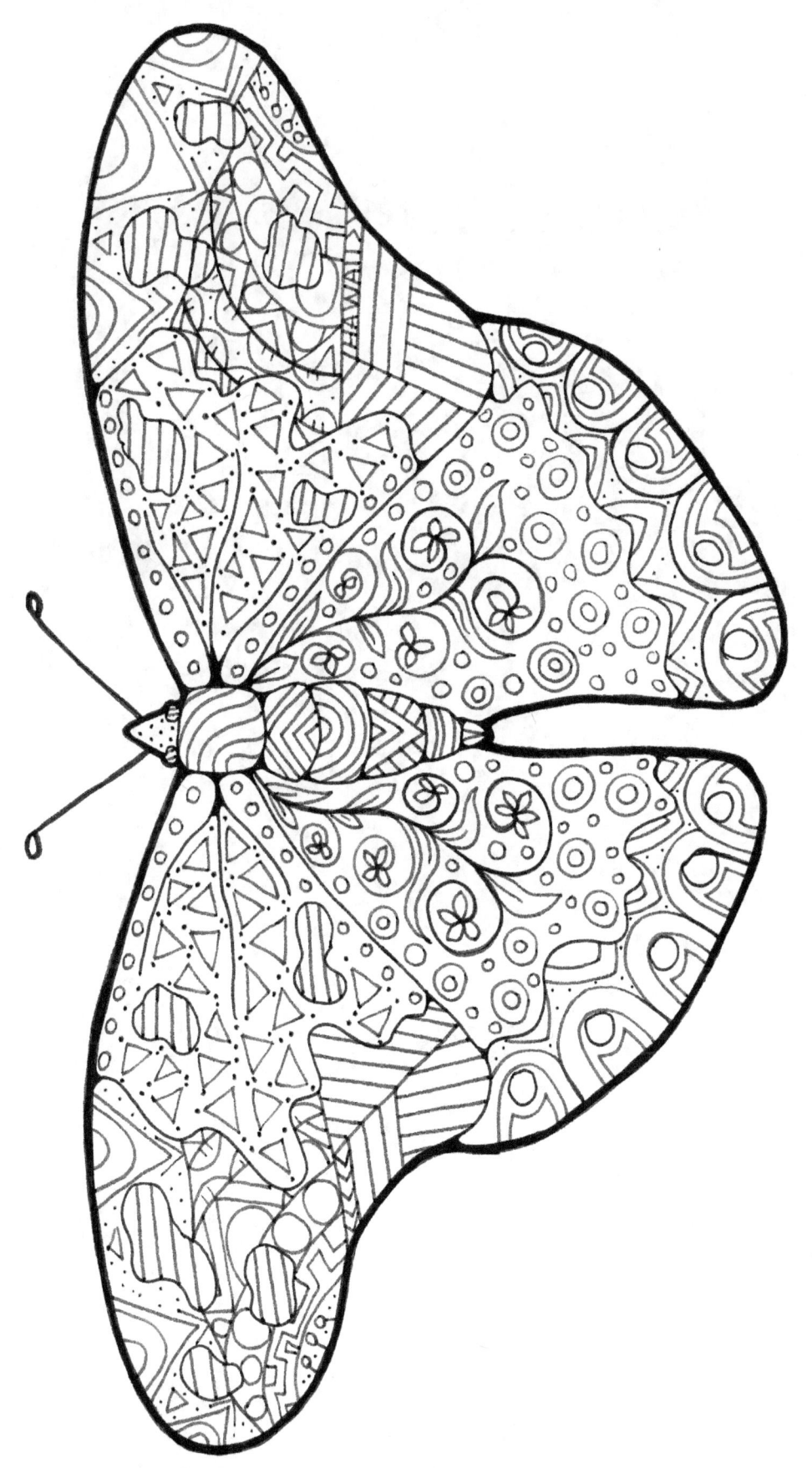

Kamehameha Butterfly

The Kamehameha butterfly is Hawaii's state insect;
Pulelehua is its name in Hawaiian

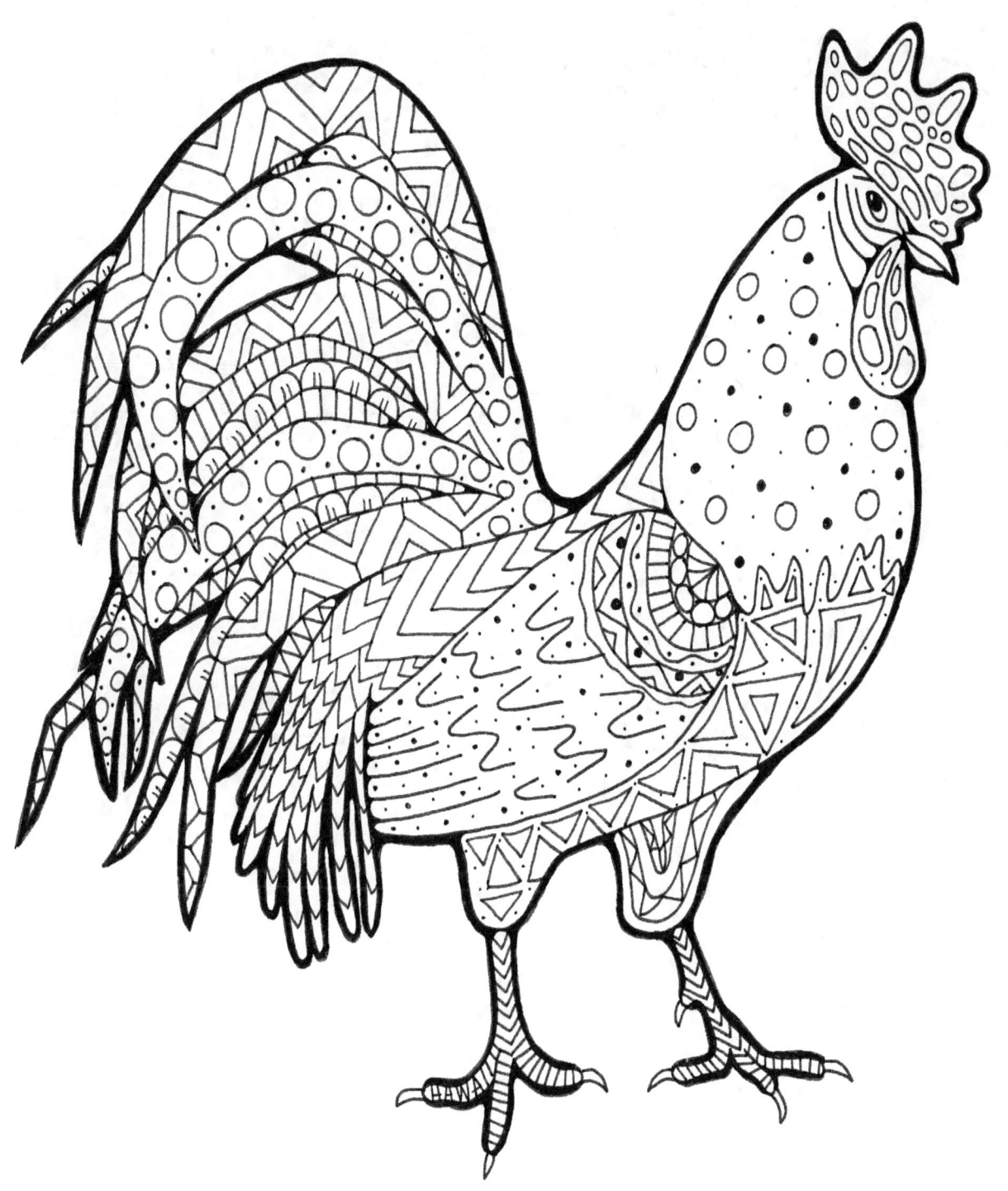

Rooster

Feral roosters and chickens are a growing problem on some of the Hawaiian islands, most notably on Kaua'i

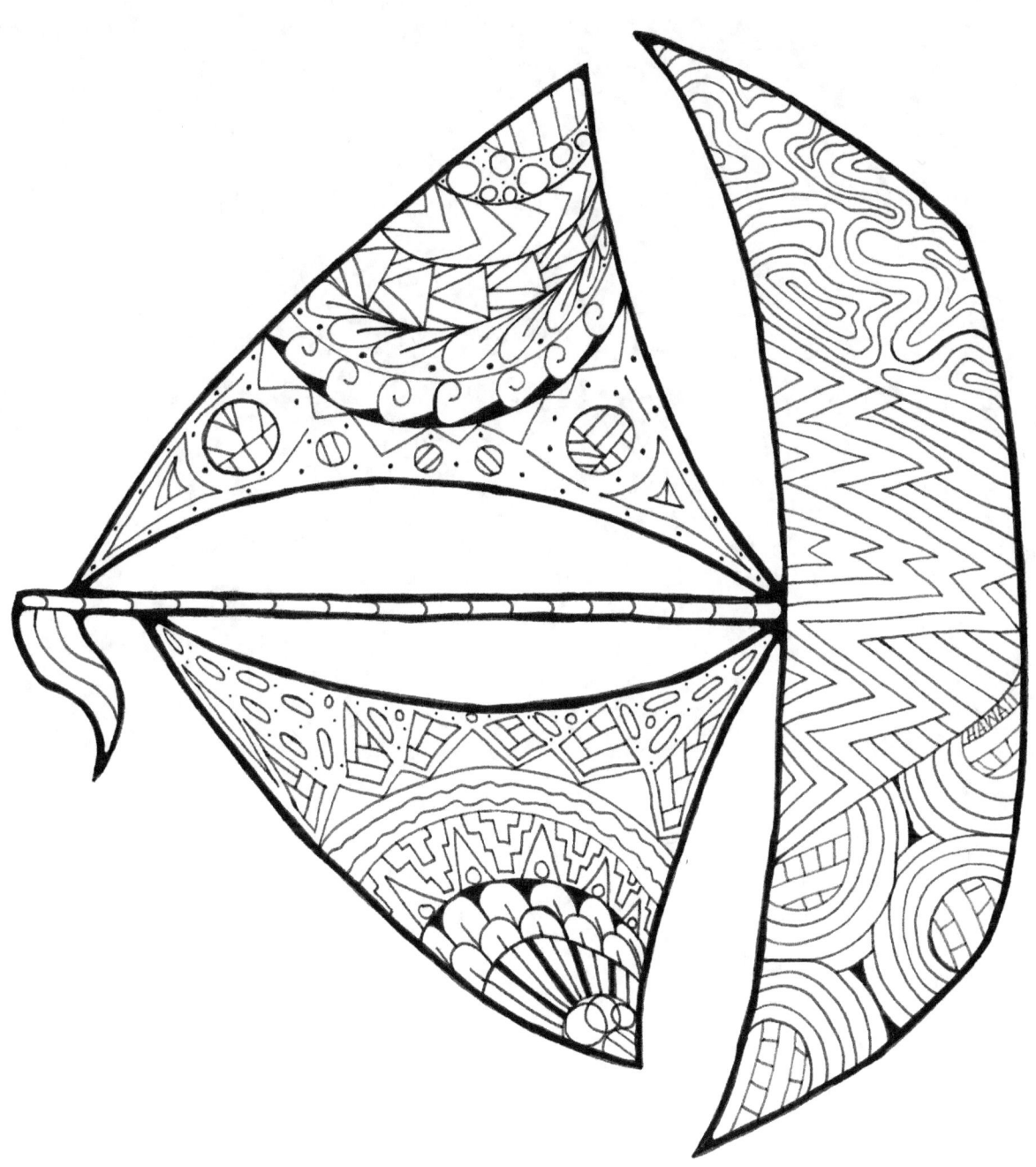

Sailing

Hawaii is an ideal place to sail year-round

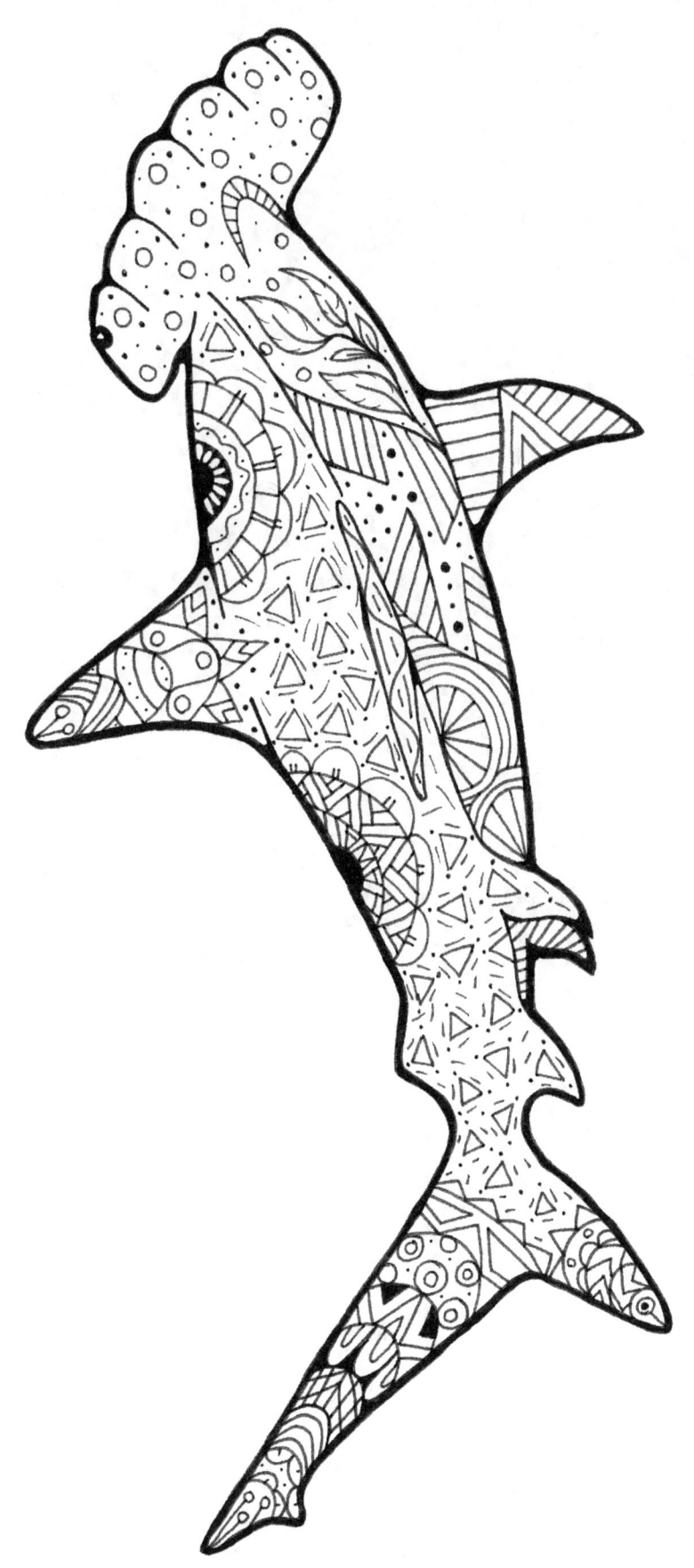

Scalloped Hammerhead Shark

Adult scalloped hammerhead sharks reach about 6-8 feet in length around the Hawaiian islands

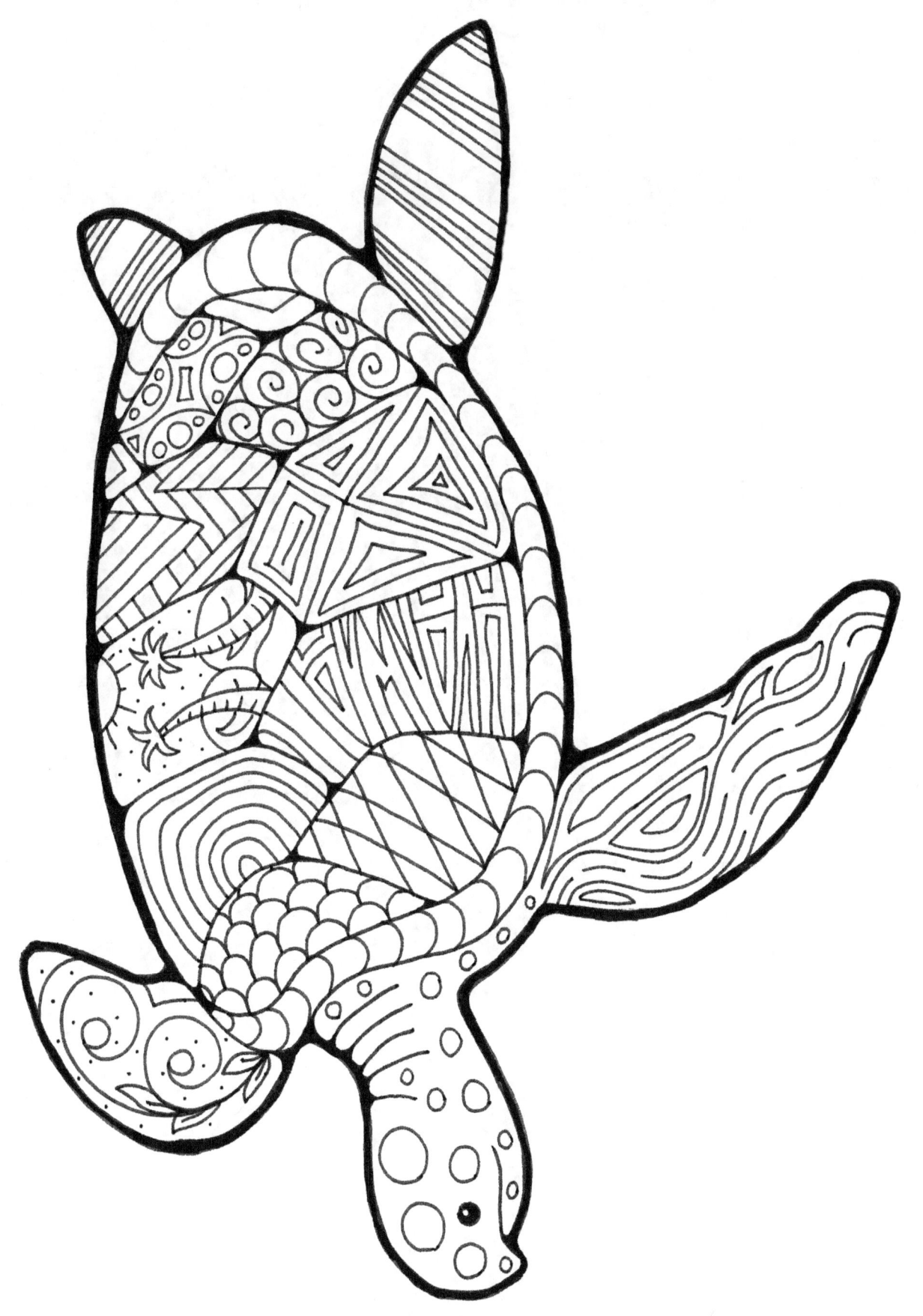

Hawaiian Sea Turtle

Known as "honu" in Hawaiian, these creatures are an endangered species

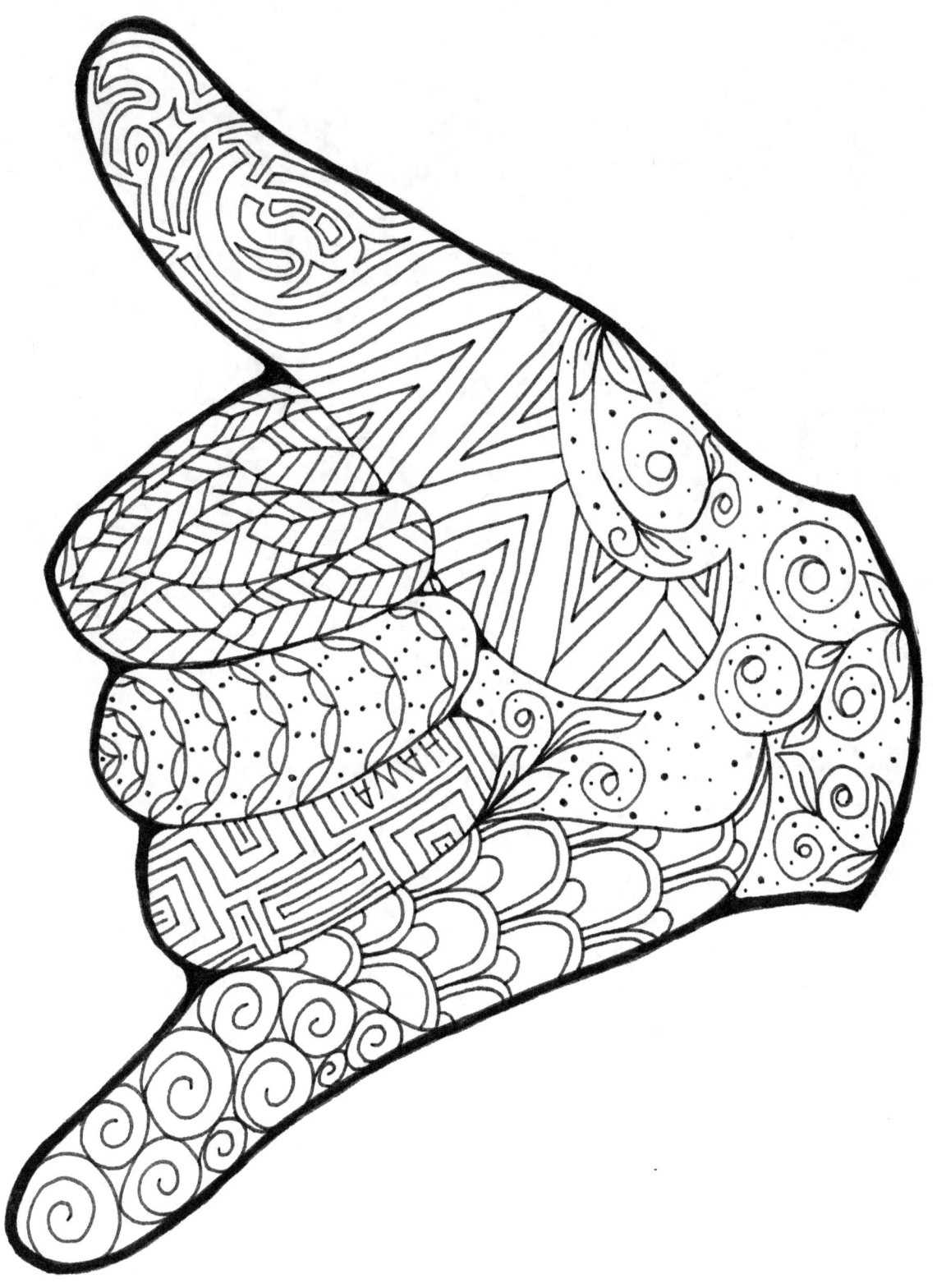

Shaka

The shaka is a friendly gesture in Hawaii

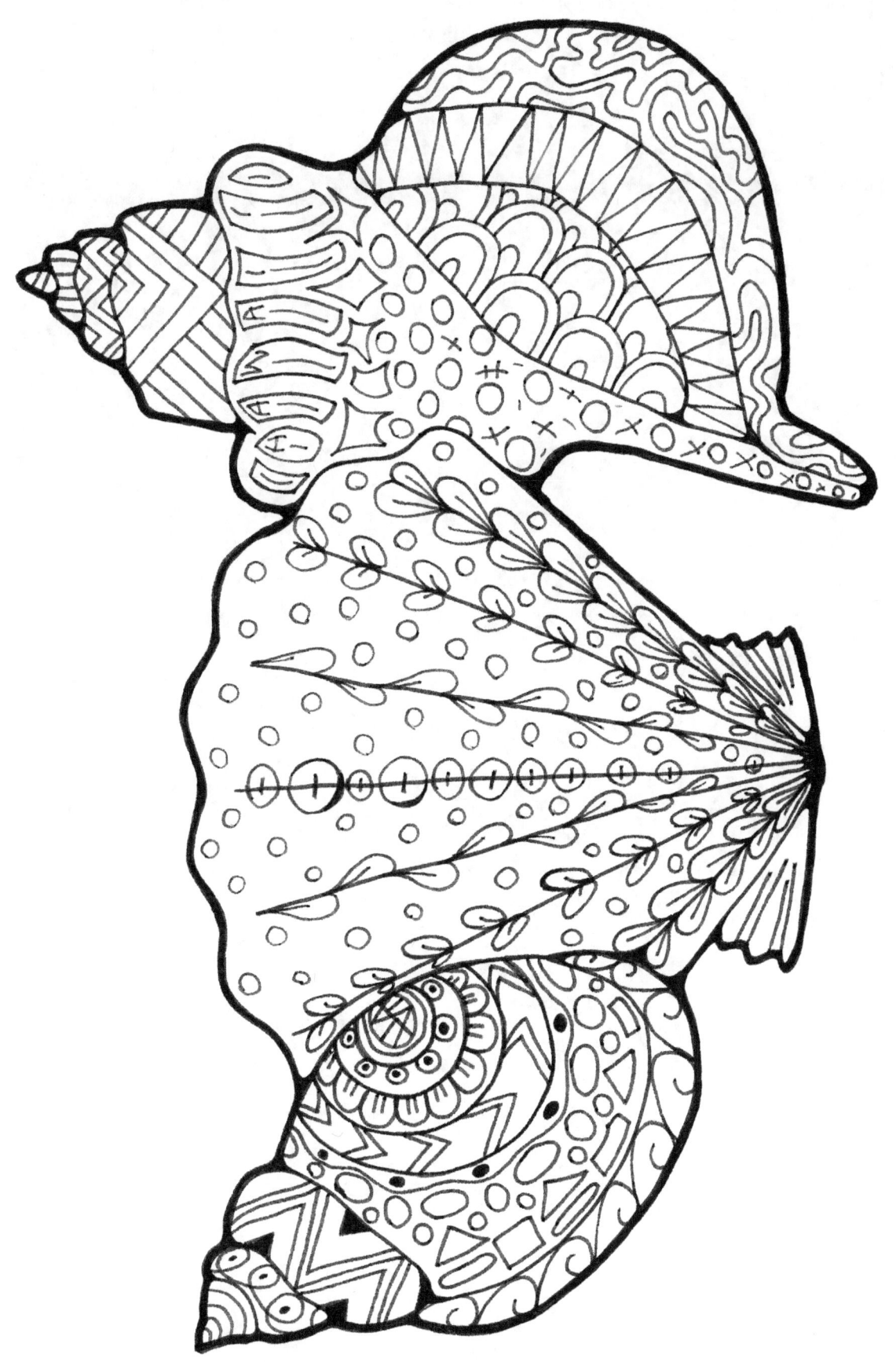

Seashells

From left to right: Tulip shell, Calico Scallop, and Conch

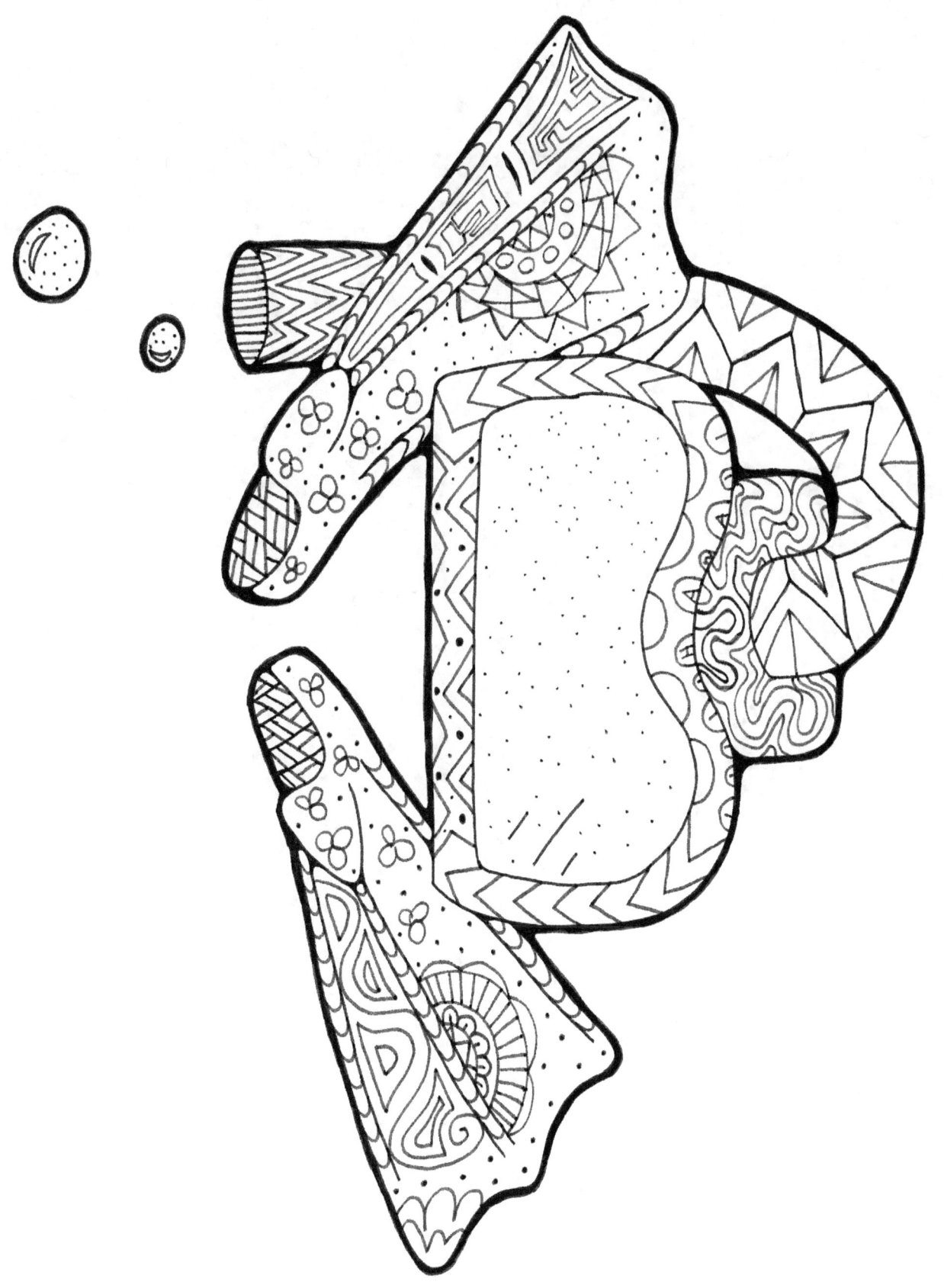

Snorkel and Flippers

Snorkeling is one of the most popular activities to do in Hawaii

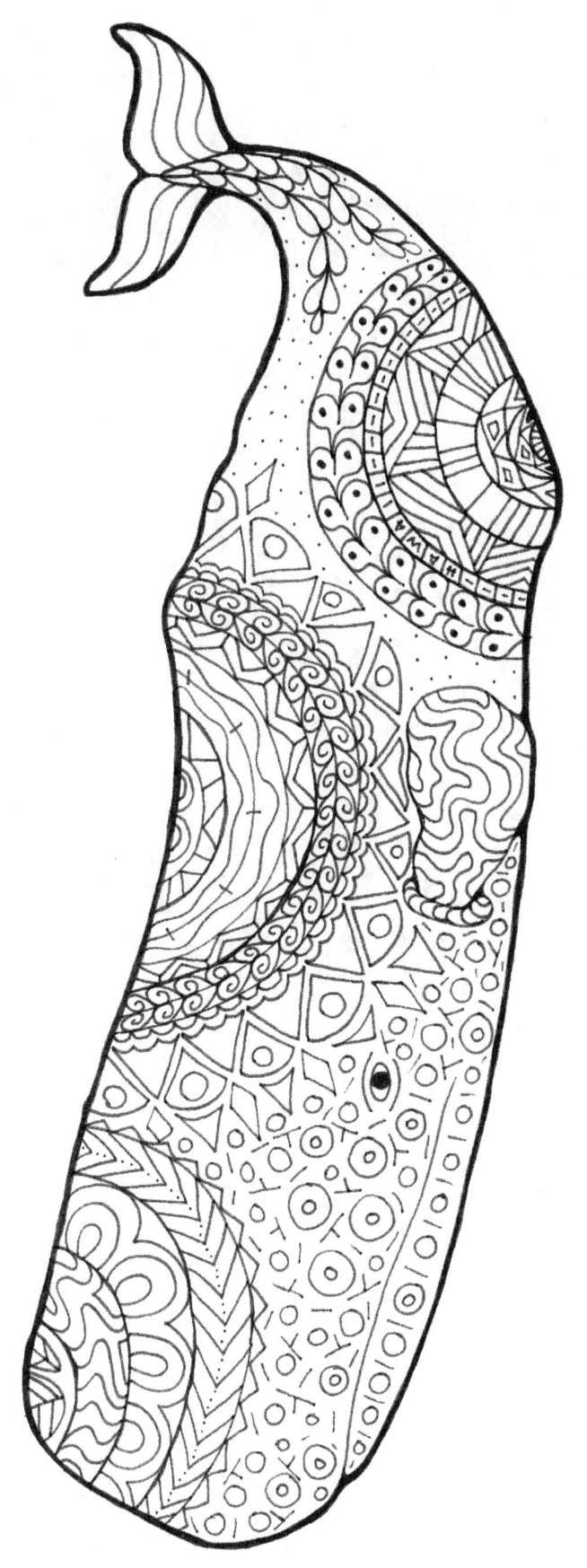

Sperm Whale

Sperm whales can dive deeper than 3,000 feet; they prefer the deeper water

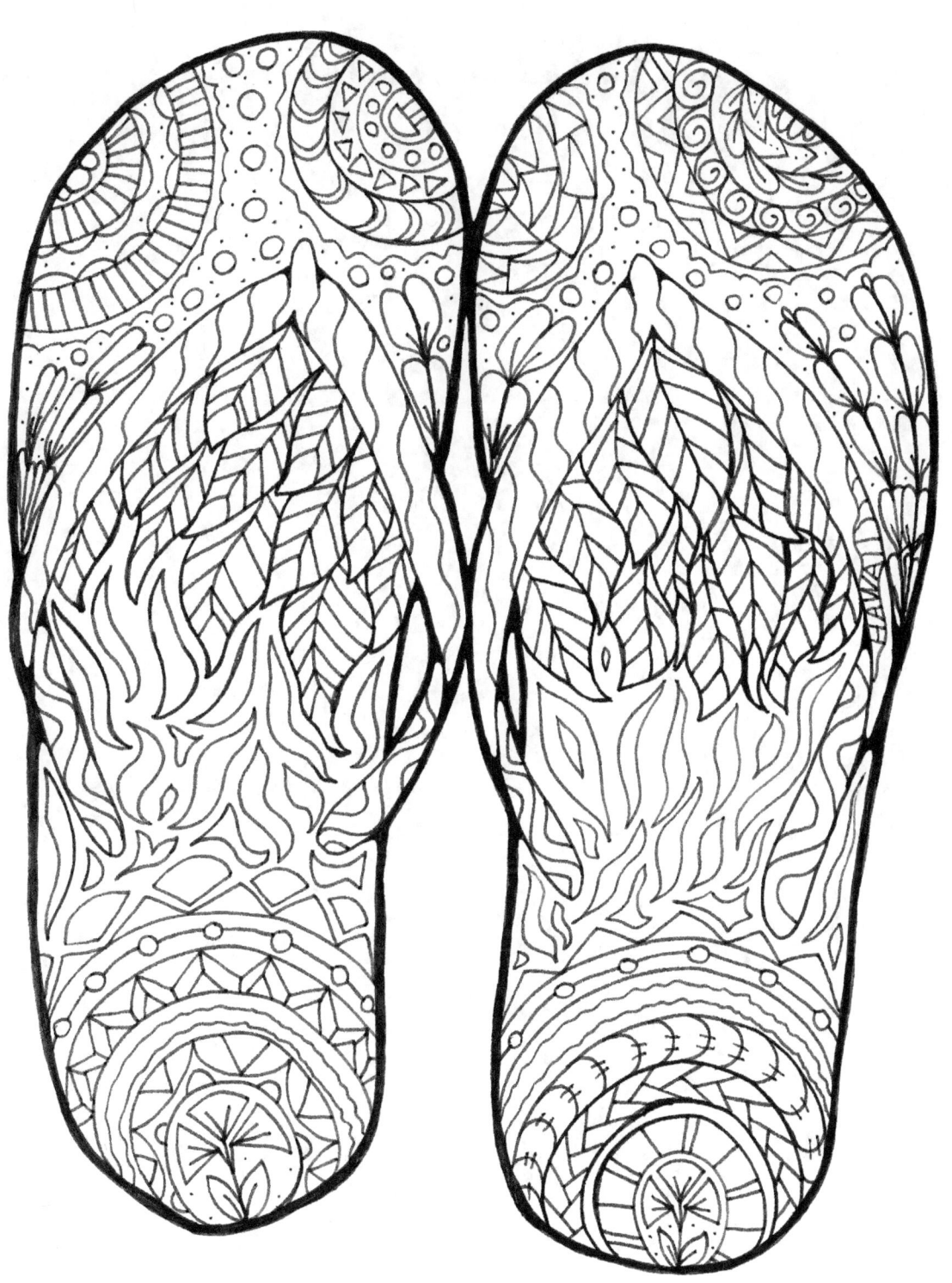

Flip Flops

Popular footwear for warm weather environments

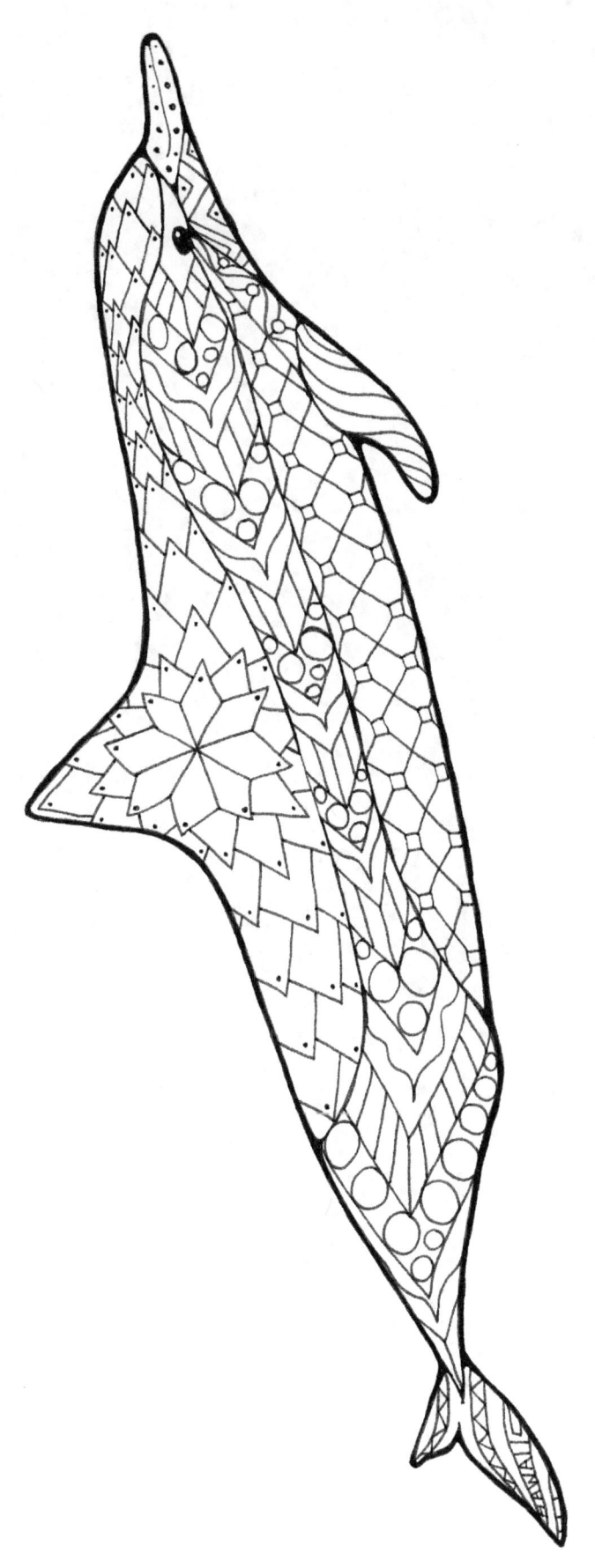

Hawaiian Spinner Dolphin

These spinner dolphins are among the most common seen in Hawaii's waters

Hawaiian: nai'a

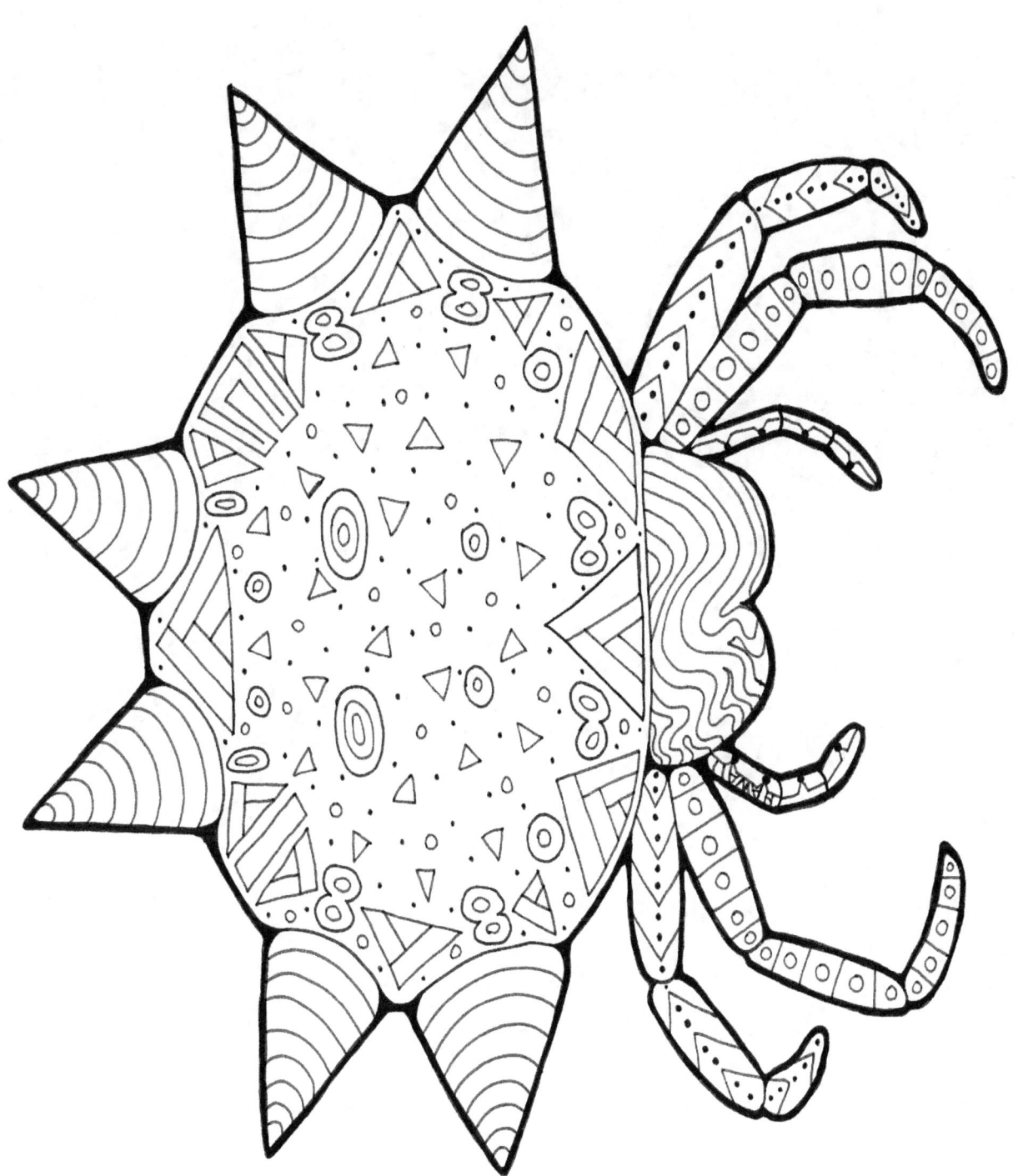

Crab Spider

Crab spider populations increase in fall and decrease later in spring

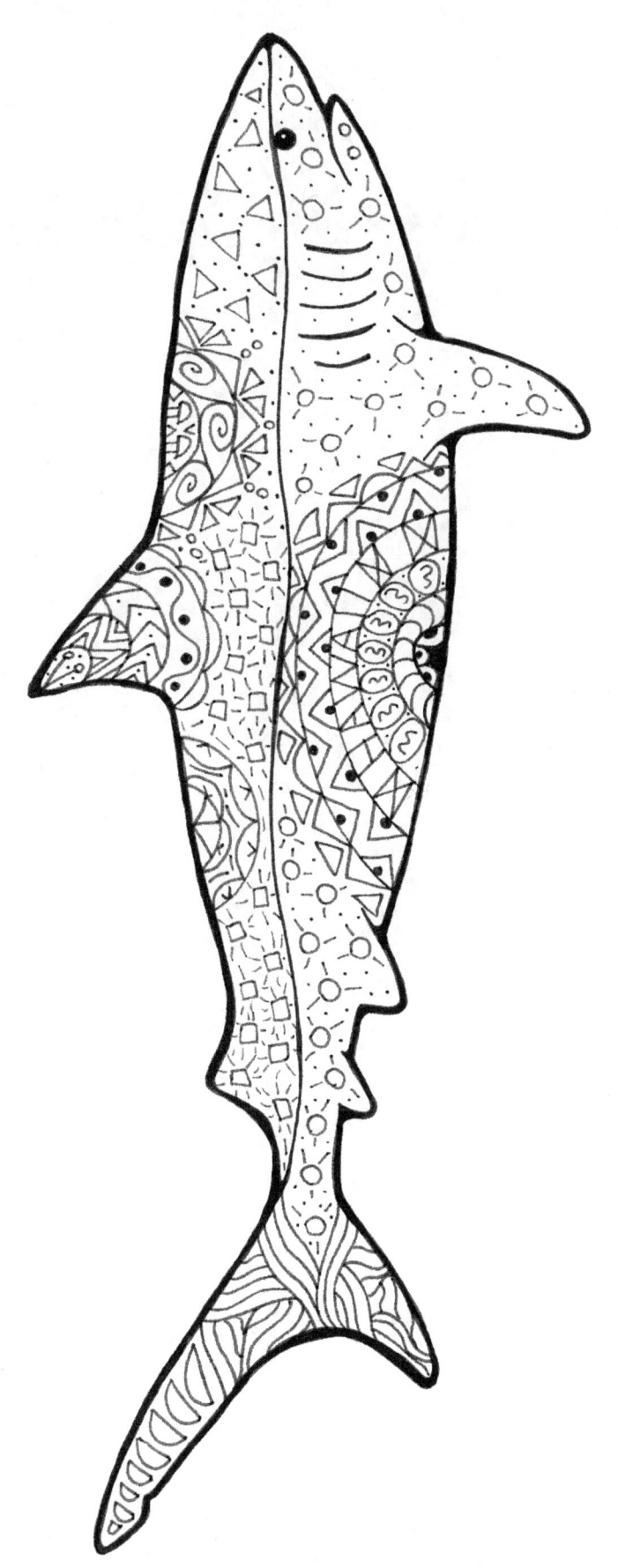

Tiger Shark

Tiger Sharks are responsible for most shark attacks in Hawaii

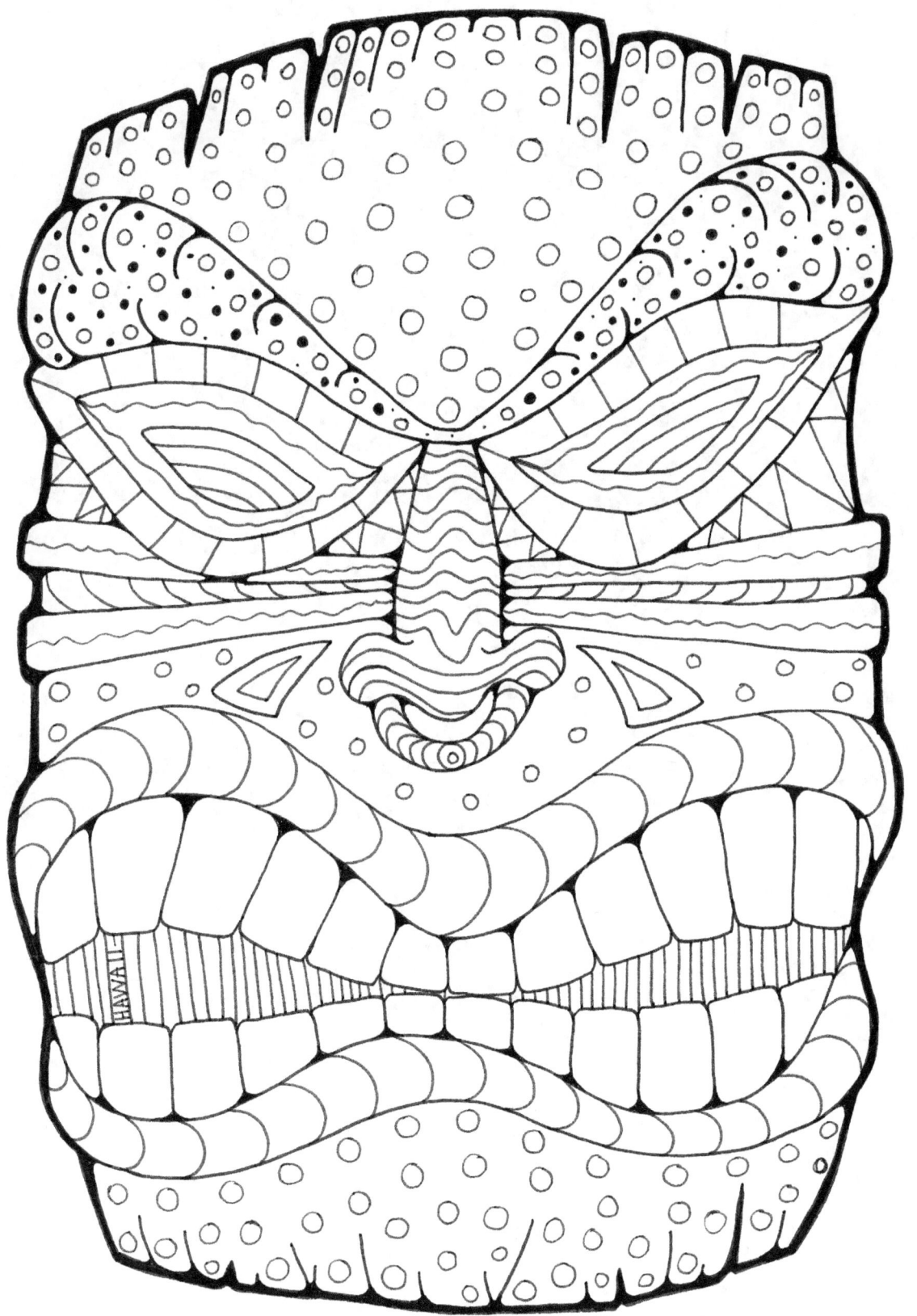

Tiki

Tikis are meant to represent the Hawaiian and Polynesian gods

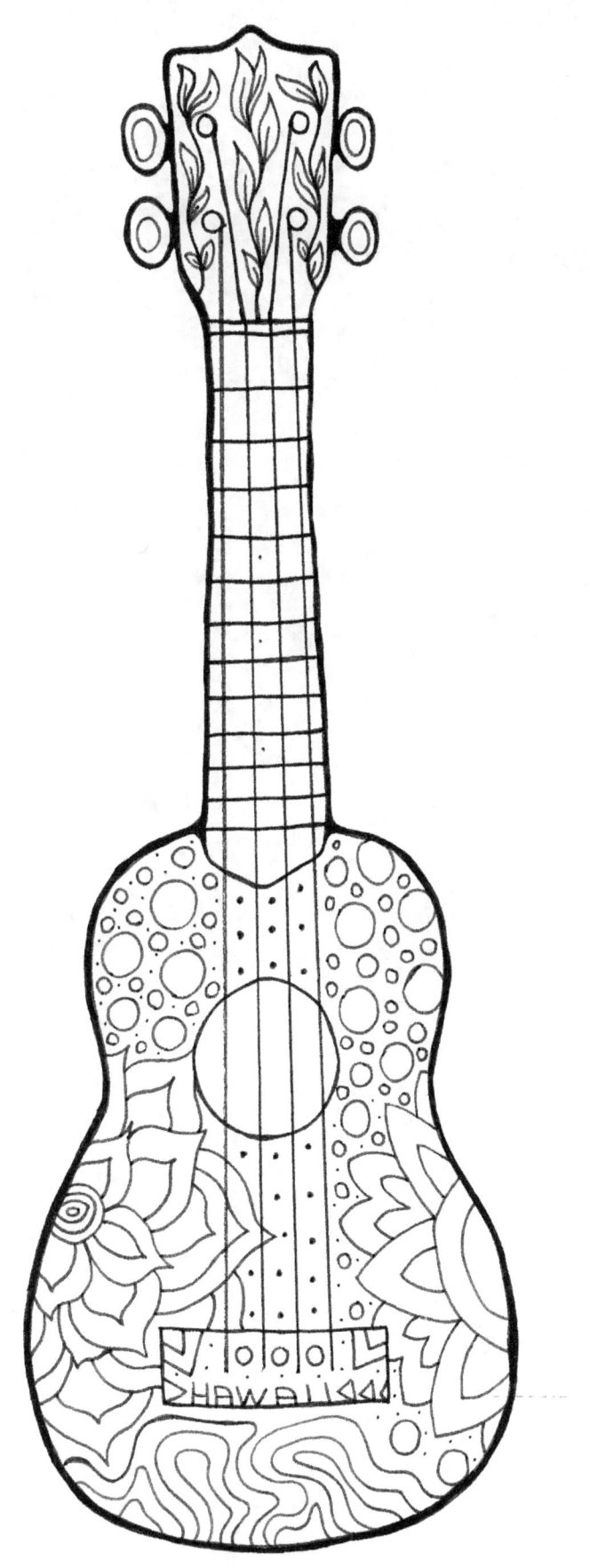

Ukulele

The ukulele was introduced to Hawaii in the 1800's

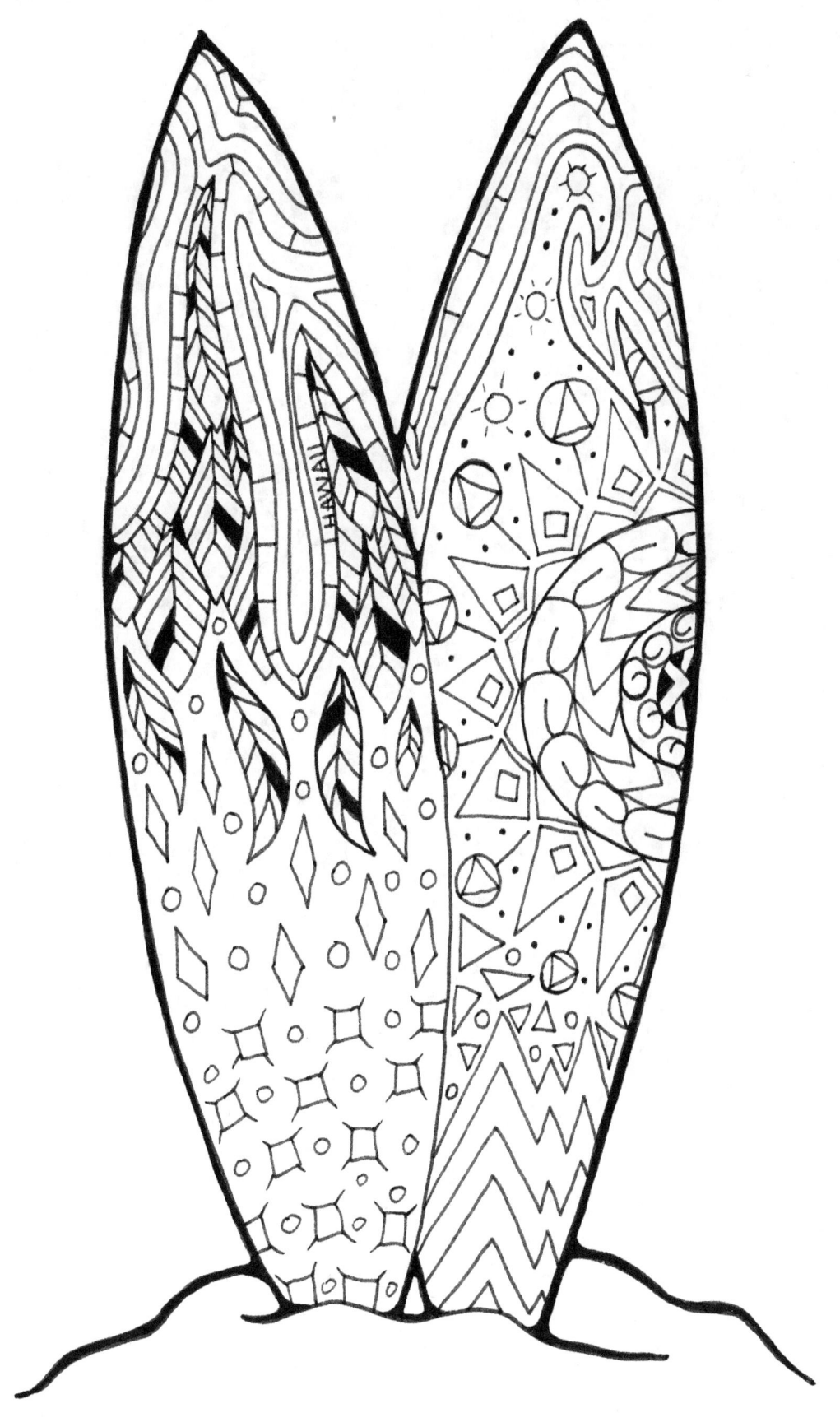

Surfing

Surfing is an iconic sport in Hawaii

Bonus Drawing:
Big Wave Surfer

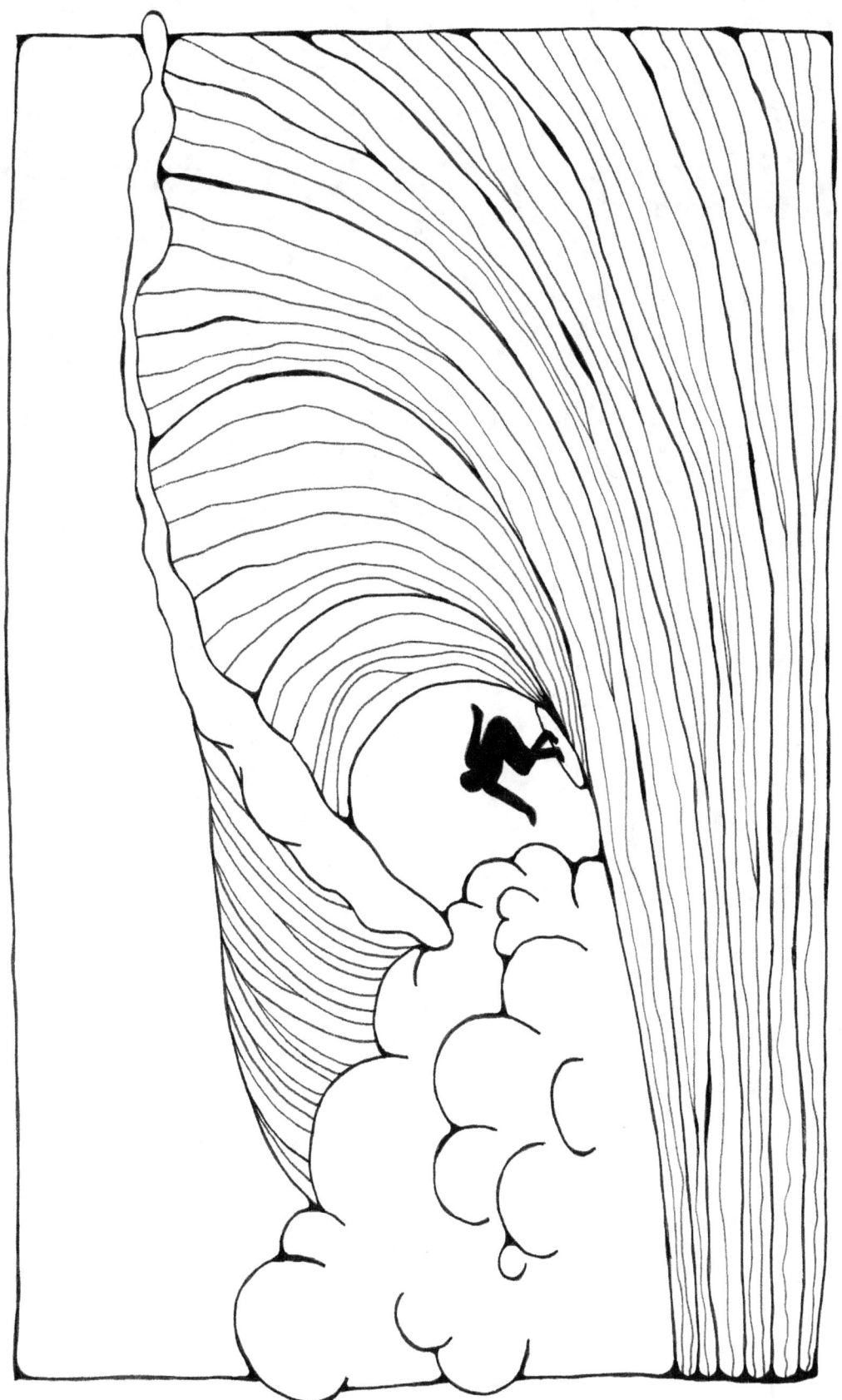

About the Artist

Brittney is a former Army brat, turned Alaskan artist from Wasilla. She lives with her partner, their daughter, and their 3 cats: Socrates, Aristotle, and Sir Frances Bacon. Brittney has always been the creative one in her family, crafting since childhood. She began drawing her animals and other special projects over 5 years ago and finds it very soothing and rewarding. She hopes you find this coloring book as fun and relaxing as she does. To keep up with her future and present projects including stickers and prints, 'like' her page on Facebook:
www.facebook.com/artbybrittneyk

If you are interested in a custom drawing or prices on art prints, please e-mail inkedfoxak@gmail.com

Finding Hawaii: A Little Help

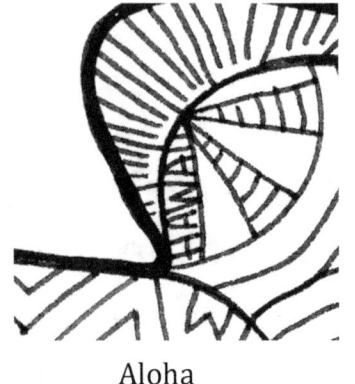

Aloha

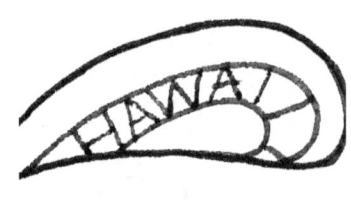

Boogie Board

Bottlenose Dolphin

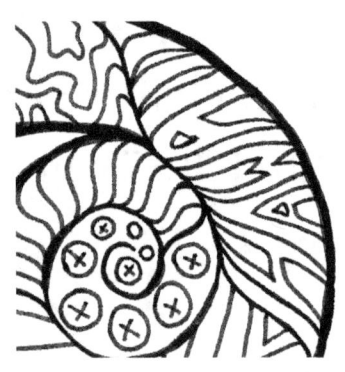

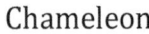

Chameleon

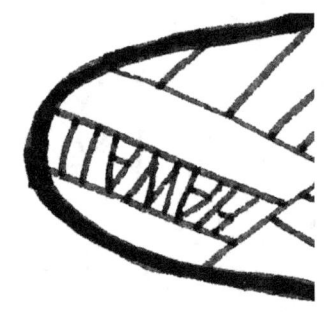

Coral

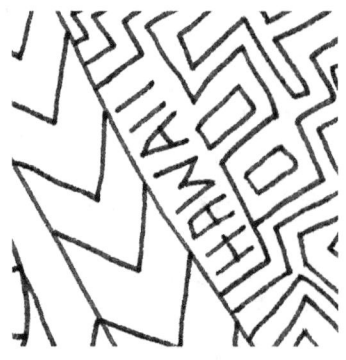

Day Octopus

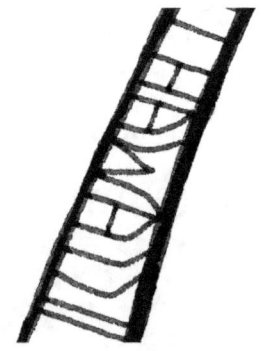

Garden Spider

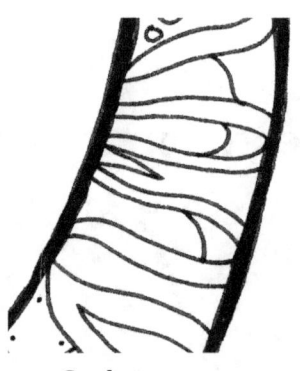

Gecko

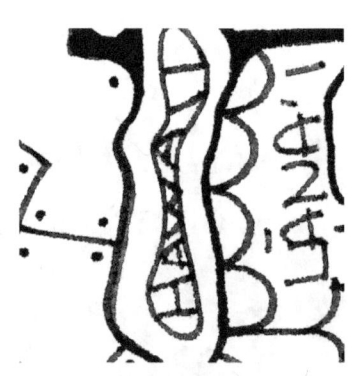

Hawaii Islands

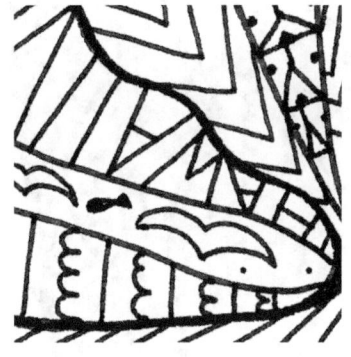

Hibiscus

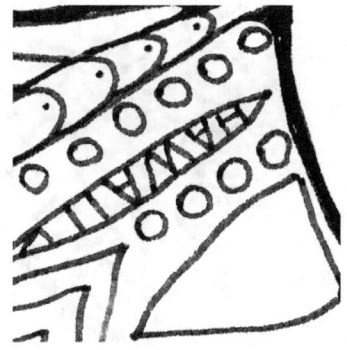

Hoary Bat

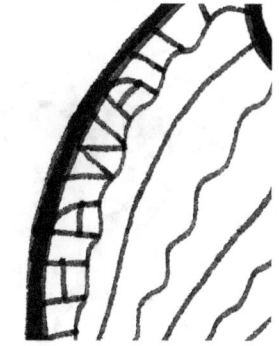

Humpback Whale

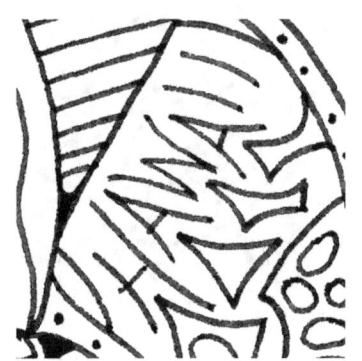

Humuhumunukunukuapua'a

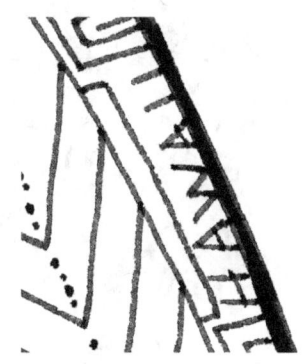

Kayak

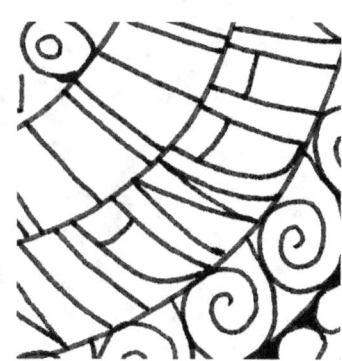

Manta Ray

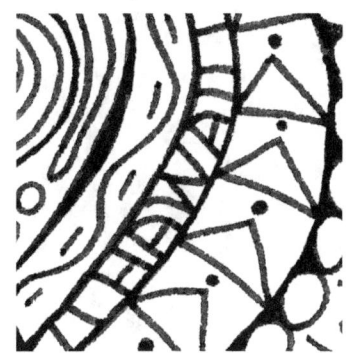

Mongoose

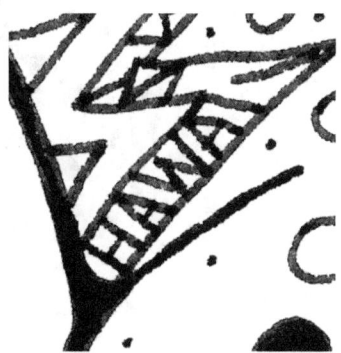

Hawaiian Monk Seal

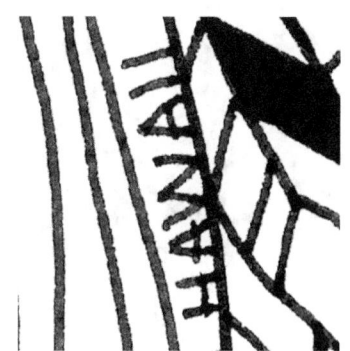

Surfboards

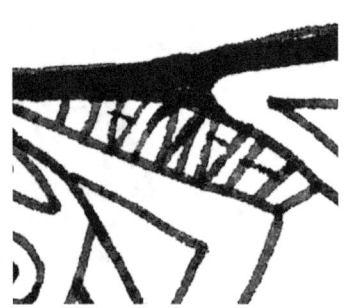
Moray Eel

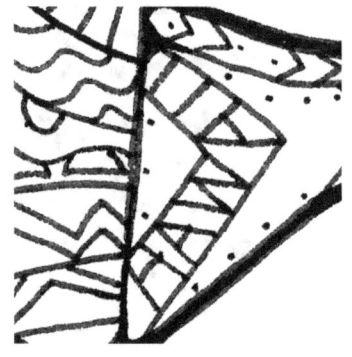
Nene

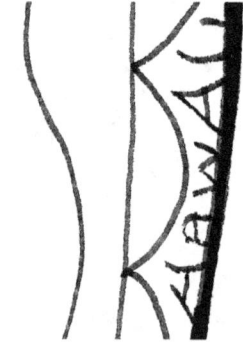
Pahu

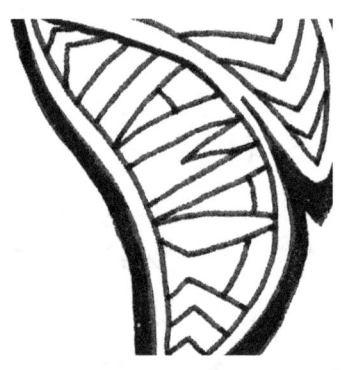
Palm Trees with Hammock

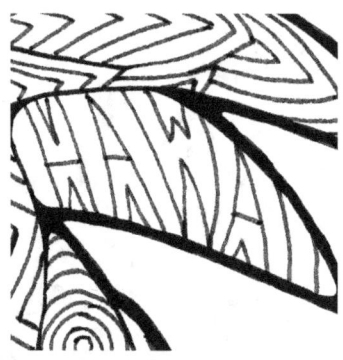
Pineapple

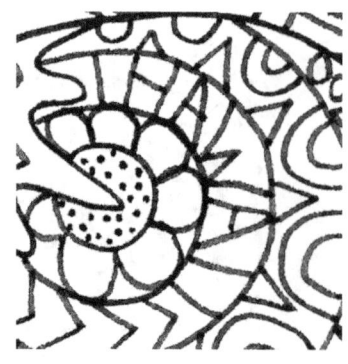
Plumeria

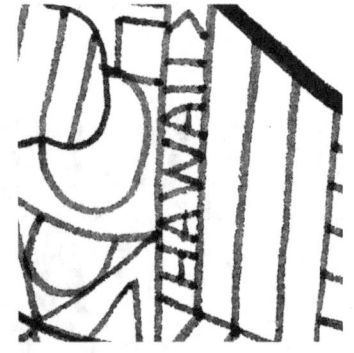
Kamehameha Butterfly

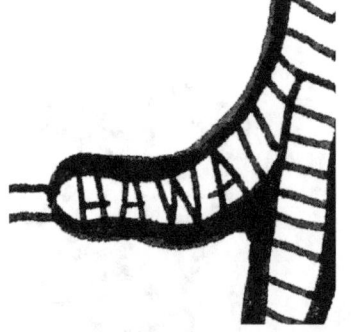
Rooster

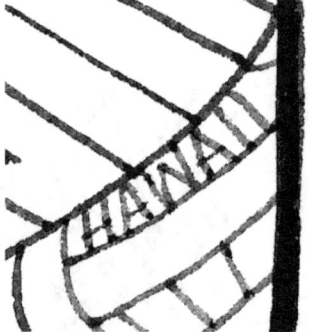
Sailboat

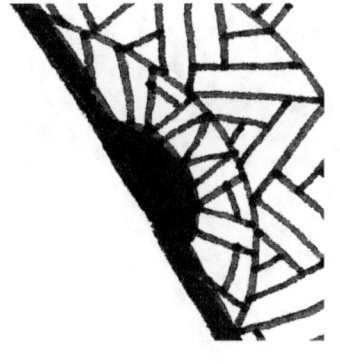

Scalloped Hammerhead Shark

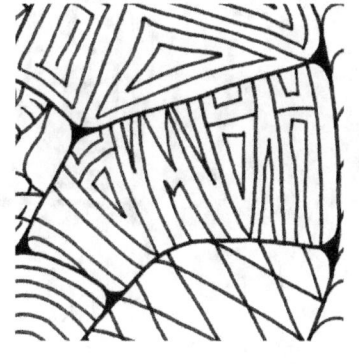

Sea Turtle

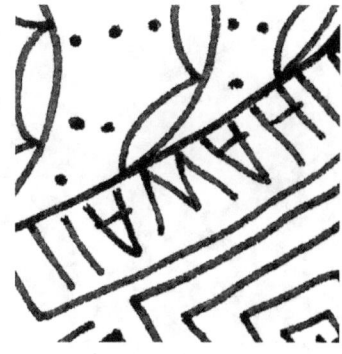

Shaka

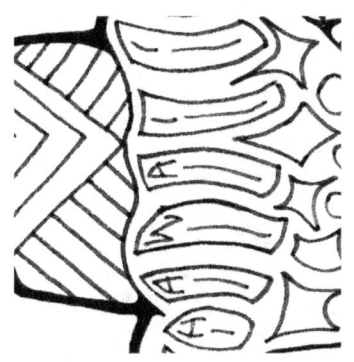

Sea Shells

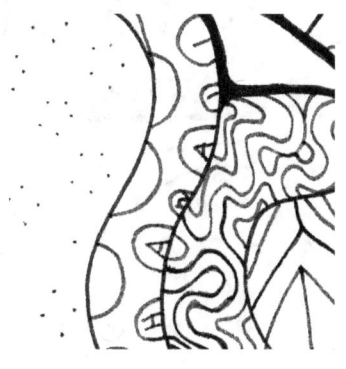

Snorkel and Flippers

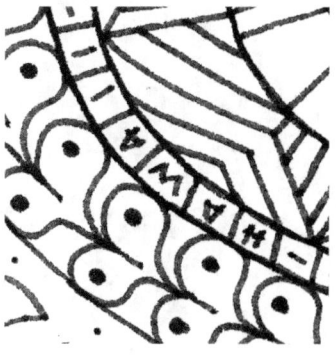

Sperm Whale

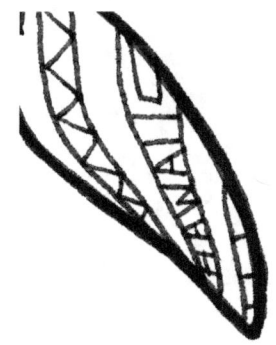

Spinner Dolphin

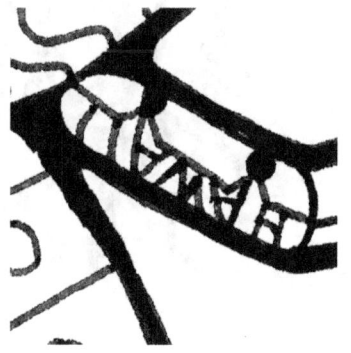

Crab Spider

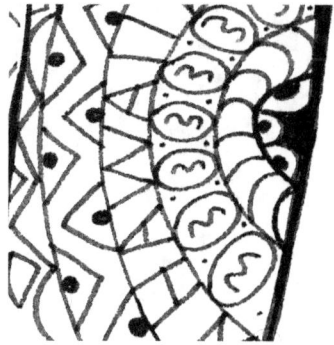

Tiger Shark

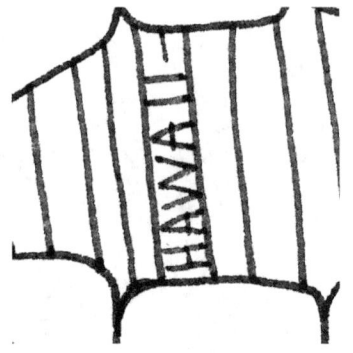

Tiki

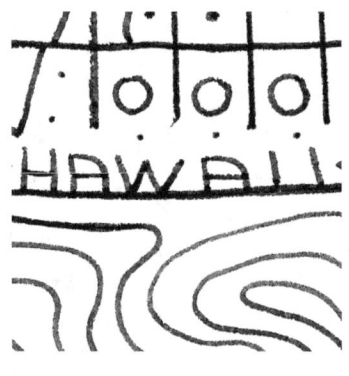

Ukulele

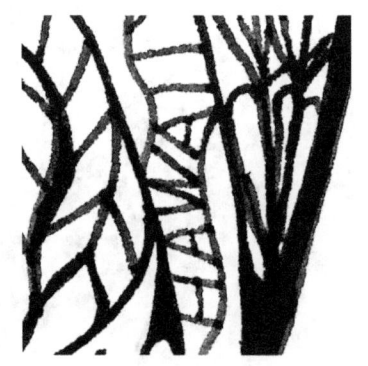

Flip Flops